Good With Money

Emma Edwards

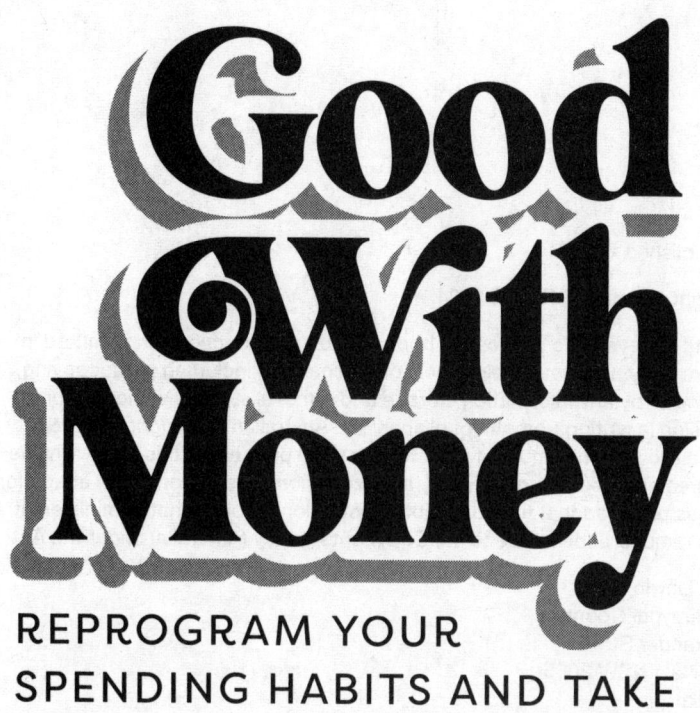

Good With Money

REPROGRAM YOUR
SPENDING HABITS AND TAKE
CONTROL OF YOUR MONEY

Emma Edwards

ALLEN&UNWIN
SYDNEY · MELBOURNE · AUCKLAND · LONDON

First published in 2024

Copyright © Emma Edwards 2024

All rights reserved. No part of this book may be reproduced or transmitted in any form or by any means, electronic or mechanical, including photocopying, recording or by any information storage and retrieval system, without prior permission in writing from the publisher. The Australian *Copyright Act 1968* (the Act) allows a maximum of one chapter or 10 per cent of this book, whichever is the greater, to be photocopied by any educational institution for its educational purposes provided that the educational institution (or body that administers it) has given a remuneration notice to the Copyright Agency (Australia) under the Act.

Allen & Unwin
Cammeraygal Country
83 Alexander Street
Crows Nest NSW 2065
Australia
Phone: (61 2) 8425 0100
Email: info@allenandunwin.com
Web: www.allenandunwin.com

Allen & Unwin acknowledges the Traditional Owners of the Country on which we live and work. We pay our respects to all Aboriginal and Torres Strait Islander Elders, past and present.

 A catalogue record for this book is available from the National Library of Australia

ISBN 978 1 76106 974 1

Set in 11/18 pt Sabon, Australia
Printed and bound in Australia by the Opus Group

10 9 8 7 6 5 4 3 2 1

 The paper in this book is FSC® certified. FSC® promotes environmentally responsible, socially beneficial and economically viable management of the world's forests.

*For anyone who's ever said
'I really need to be better with money'.
Let's take that off your to-do list.*

Contents

Good With Money ix

Part 1   Give yourself a break

Cellulite cream and cabbage soup 3
Impossible standards 6
'Are you wearing the—' 'Chanel boots? Yeah, I am.' 11
The playground of consumption 17
The rise of social media 28
What keeps us spending 44
There's simply too much to spend money on 58

Part 2   Get out of your own way

Our irrational brains 63
Emotional spending 66
Our financial experiences and perspectives 72
Our self-worth and identity 86
Our relationship with money 93
Meeting your inner villains 96

Part 3   Taking back your power

Getting back in the driver's seat 107
Getting financially aware 115

Confronting your toxic financial beliefs	140
Engaging with money in a more positive way	157
Reclaiming your financial decisions	166
Relearning how to spend money	176
Values-based spending	191
Finding your why	204

Part 4 Putting it all into practice

Active and intentional money management	213
Your financial ecosystem: the Good With Money method	218
Sticking to your money management system	244
How to keep your habits in check	256
Intuitive money management	263

Part 5 Get ready for the rest of your life

Becoming the main character of your money	269
Ongoing work on your money beliefs and financial comfort zone	278
Building financial resilience	286
Cultivating a positive relationship with money	293
Earning more, building wealth and creating a life of freedom	298
Go out there and be Good With Money!	311

Acknowledgements	317

Good With Money

Good With Money is a label that we all want to wear. You probably know someone who others would describe as Good With Money—perhaps a sibling or a friend. If you're reading this book, it's probably not how you'd describe yourself. But that's all about to change.

For as long as I can remember, I was a hot mess with money. I didn't have a juicy savings balance, I'd constantly fear looking at my bank accounts and I often wondered where the heck all my money went. It honestly felt like every time I left the house I'd return $100 worse off. I'd try to set budgets, I'd make grand claims about how I was going to start saving money and be one of 'those' people who have it all together. But every single time, I'd end up back where I started, or worse. Living pay cheque to pay cheque, constantly running into unexpected expenses, taking one step forward and two steps back and throwing the towel in when it got too overwhelming. I just couldn't get ahead. I'd hear people described as Good With Money and a distinct twinge of shame, panic and guilt would rush over me, because I knew I was the absolute antithesis of that celebrated ideal.

But now, I can say I *am* one of those people. I can say I'm Good With Money—and you're going to be able to say the same after implementing the learnings in this book. It was a slow process at first, but over time, I managed to master my habits, dig deep into my behaviour and the emotions that went with it, and gradually, things started to change.

In this book, I will talk about money in ways you might not have considered before. We'll look at why it's actually really hard to be Good With Money and the barriers you need to overcome to change your finances once and for all. I'll help you to reframe your financial perspective so you can see money differently, understand yourself better, build habits that you can actually stick to and, ultimately, start feeling like you're in the driver's seat of your finances.

Good With Money will take you on a journey of self-discovery and teach you the why behind your own financial challenges. We'll look at why it's so hard to keep track of where your money goes (spoiler: it's not your fault), why you're so emotionally entangled with money, how your upbringing can impact your financial behaviour and the cycles that keep you stuck.

Then we'll get down to business. You'll learn to reclaim your decision-making, stop wondering where your money went, quit wishing you could go back in time and undo all your spending from the weekend, and start managing money in a way that makes sense and makes you feel good.

What being Good With Money is not

Before we dive in, I want to touch on what being Good With Money is not. You see, there exists this blurry line between being Good With Money and being really frugal.

Being Good With Money isn't about how much you've got in your savings or whether or not you shop at the two-dollar store. It's not about reusing your toilet paper or never buying lunch. It's not about being wealthy (though it can certainly get you there) and it's not about being a numbers whizz.

Being Good With Money doesn't mean becoming the type of person who always packs a sandwich everywhere they go, takes public transport to save a couple of bucks, cuts their own hair and would sooner see the dark side of hell than pay for a facial.

That said, I have absolutely no issue with packing a sandwich, taking a lunch, riding public transport, cutting your own hair or opting out of certain luxuries as long as this is part of a *conscious decision* that your money is better used on other things. Essentially, being Good With Money isn't about depriving yourself or living by a rigid rulebook. Thank goodness for that, right?

What being Good With Money IS

Being Good With Money is about doing money your way. It's understanding why you do the things you do with money. It's being so deeply connected to your finances that you know how your money can best serve you. It's feeling that you control money, rather than letting money control you. It's using money to support you in the pursuit of your best life, while knowing that you've done what you can to set yourself up for the future. It's knowing how to prioritise your money to balance enjoying life now with looking after future you.

Being Good With Money means taking an active role in your finances and making the decision to be in the driver's seat. You don't need to be perfect. You can be Good With Money even if you're paying off debt. You can be Good With Money if you're going through a rough time financially. You can be Good With Money even if historically you've been everything but. You can be Good With Money on a low income, a middle income or a super juicy high income. In fact, it's in your interest to get Good With Money *before* you earn a super juicy and jacked-up high income so that you can maximise that sweet, sweet dollar.

Before we get started, I need to level with you. Learning to be Good With Money doesn't solve the gross inequities that exist in a capitalist world. It doesn't fix the broken system that denies society's most vulnerable their basic needs. It doesn't change the fact that 99 per cent of the world's wealth is hoarded by 1 per cent of the population. It doesn't change the fact that being born into generational privilege remains the most effective way to get ahead.

I have shed a lot of tears during the writing of this book for that very reason. I've questioned whether I should even write it. I really wish a book could fix the system. But while I can't give you a trust fund (how good would that be?!), what I can do is equip you with the tools and information that helped me turn my finances around by learning how to spend, save and manage my money effectively, and build up a level of financial confidence by working with the things in my control.

The aim of *Good With Money* is to give you the reddest, hottest crack at making the most of this one wonderful life that you get to lead. I want to set you free from money anxiety and shame, give you control over your circumstances, help you make the best decisions you can with the information and resources you have, and get you unstuck and off that financial hamster wheel once and for all.

I've broken this book down into five parts. In Part 1, we delve into the external world, and explore the ways we're held back from financial confidence by everything from diet culture to advertising to social media. Then, in Part 2 we'll go inwards, exploring how your baked-in factory settings get in the way of your being Good With Money. Part 3 is all about taking back your power, confronting your sabotaging money patterns and reprogramming the way you think and behave. In Part 4, I'll teach you how to build your own financial ecosystem using the Good With Money method, and you'll learn the practical systems and structures you need to keep your new habits going. And in Part 5, we'll look ahead to the rest of your life, and explore how your new Good With Money status can open doors to things you never believed were possible for you.

So why am I the person to take you on this journey? Firstly, I know what it's like to feel as though you'll be a hot money mess forever, and I've been on the journey of turning my finances around myself. But I've also spent the last five years talking about money online, helping people uncover the why behind their financial behaviour and improve their relationship with money.

I've taught over a thousand people how to build positive money habits in my masterclasses and workbooks, built a following of over sixty thousand people on social media, and had the privilege of being in the ears of thousands of listeners every week via The Broke Generation podcast. My obsession with the emotional, psychological and behavioural aspects of money then led me to undertake graduate study in Financial Psychology and Behavioural Finance, and obtain a designation as a Certified Financial Behavior Specialist® (FBS).

Trust me when I say this stuff is my true passion. I want to help as many people feel Good With Money as I possibly can, and it's my hope that this book is the resource that'll change your finances for good.

Before we begin: a question

Imagine that tonight, while you were sleeping, a miracle occurred and you woke up able to say you were Good With Money. What would be different? How would you notice the change had occurred? How would you feel? How would your life be enriched?

Grab a notebook or open your notes app and write down anything that pops up for you when you think about this. Don't worry about right or wrong. This question is designed to help you think about money in a different way, outside of the numbers and the practical stuff, and tap into what money means to you, and the life that awaits you on the other side of this book.

Keep that notebook or notes app handy—some parts of this book contain exercises or reflections that you'll wanna scribble down.

PART 1

Give yourself a break

The very first step to becoming Good With Money is to give yourself a fucking break. And I mean that in absolute earnest.

There is so much 'should' and 'shouldn't' when it comes to money. We *should* be saving, we *shouldn't* be buying that, we *should* only be spending this percentage of our salary, we *shouldn't* feel so down about house prices.

The result of all this shoulding and shouldn'ting is a big steaming pile of shitty shame. And we don't ever want you feeling any kind of shame about money, so rest assured, this book is not about guilting you into doing things differently.

In Part 1, I'm going to give us all the break we need by talking through some of the many factors that explain why we find it hard to be Good With Money. From modern technology to the media to advertising strategies—there are a myriad of things that get in the way of our attempts to master money. Some of these things you might've considered before, other things might blow your mind and have you going, 'OH MY GOD, THAT MAKES SO MUCH SENSE.' And

I'm not going to lie, there will be parts that make you angry. Rage is hot—embrace it.

But what this section is aiming to do is make you breathe a big sigh of relief. Relief that, hang on, it's not actually your fault, you're not broken, you're not an entitled brat who's been getting it wrong all these years (despite what boomer media might tell us). And after you breathe that sigh of relief, you're going to be fired right up to get Good With Money on your own terms.

Cellulite cream and cabbage soup

For a huge portion of my life, I could rattle off the number of calories in a Mars bar, tell you which type of pumpkin had the least carbs and regale you with my reviews of different diet teas, but I had no idea what my bank balance was, or what was in my savings account. Actually, I probably could've told you what was in my savings account, because it was sweet fucking nothing.

I was born in 1991, and as anyone else who grew up in the nineties will know, diet culture was everything and everywhere. Carbs were the devil, low-rise jeans cuddled our belly fat and everything that entered our mouths could be reduced down to good or bad, on-plan or off-plan, worthy or unworthy.

I'm an only child and I was raised by a single mother. Since it was just the two of us, I was always a bit more of a grown-up than a kid—probably because there was less separation between the adults and the children, and more just me and my mum making it work on our own. One thing I remember clearly is that so much of what we ate was defined by the diet that was in vogue at the time. The Cabbage Soup Diet, WeightWatchers, Slimming World, calorie counting, whatever the stars of popular soaps were rattling off in their 'what I eat on set' interviews with the weekly gossip magazines. Like many women, I was, by extension, either on a diet or aware of dieting before I'd even hit puberty.

You're probably thinking three things right now.

1. Thanks for the reminder of that hellish time.
2. Isn't it wild how the stench of cabbage soup never really leaves you?
3. What the fuck does this have to do with money?

Great question. Actually, a lot.

The healthy eating, nutrition and weight loss sector that's become known as the 'wellness economy' was valued at $946 billion in 2020. And it's growing. If you thought diet culture died with Justin and Britney's relationship, think again. Capitalism's cash cow is alive and well.

In fact, while we've been busy posting #bodyacceptance quotes, the diet industry has been working on an almighty yet subtle rebrand. Over the last decade or so, analysts have been tracking the diet industry's pivot from 'diets' to 'health', and they can tell you that it's working. When it comes to making money, it doesn't matter whether it's a weight loss shake or a meal delivery service promising healthy, balanced meals for the busy woman; the first step is always to convince us that there's something wrong with us, in order to sell us a solution. And that right there is what all of this has to do with being Good With Money.

For far too long, our priorities have been misdirected and manipulated for profit. We spent our formative years being told that nothing tastes as good as skinny feels. That a moment on the lips means a lifetime on the hips. That showing cellulite in public is the ultimate sin. And that the only numbers worth caring about are the ones on the scale, the ones on the label of our jeans, and the ones on the back of the packet.

We've been told that what's important is how much we weigh, how long our eyelashes are, how many steps we do in a day, how much cellulite we have, how to get the guy, dressing for our body type (shoutout to my fellow pears) and who is still in the running towards becoming America's Next Top Model (okay, this one actually did matter).

What we weren't ever encouraged to care about were things like being happy, understanding wealth or retirement or business, prioritising money, compound interest or building financial security.

Impossible standards

I want to take a brief journey back in time to talk about female financial participation. Historically, women have been denied financial autonomy in countless ways. In Australia, women couldn't get a bank loan without a male guarantor until 1971. Until 1966, married women weren't permitted to remain in the workforce after marriage. In the UK, women couldn't open a bank account in their own name until 1975. In Ireland, women couldn't own their own home outright without a man until 1976.

Over the years these formal restrictions have unwound, and for a lot of us reading this book, all we've ever known is the degree of financial autonomy that we have today. We can get our own jobs, open our own bank accounts, and rent or own our own homes (costs aside). But despite legislative changes to financial practices, the patriarchy still keeps a watchful eye over where our money goes by finding ways to consistently move the goalposts on what a woman should be. The feminine ideal went from mother to career woman, object of the male gaze to 'one of the blokes', housewife to girlboss. No matter what, there is always a standard to live up to. These ever-changing standards manufacture an endless list of problems, for which there is always a fix available for purchase.

Effectively, we're conditioned to hand our money right back to the patriarchy by paying for the new range of diet products, buying male-owned women's magazines to see whose cellulite looked the worst on their summer holiday or find out what Jo from S Club 7 ate in a day, or shopping the trending style because it promised to slim our waists.

The collateral damage: our self-worth and our net worth

Billion-dollar industries aside, there's more to the money side of our diet-fuelled childhoods than meets the eye. Growing up in the toxic era of diet culture that ravaged the eighties, nineties and noughties, under the ever-changing standards of what a woman should be, many of us developed a deeply damaged view of ourselves and our worth. In some cases, that has also had a huge effect on the way we see money.

Convincing an entire gender that their value lies in their thinness and their appearance was one of the patriarchy's more lucrative ideas. Create the problem, sell the solution. Bingo.

Because where our focus goes, our money flows. If you love art, you've probably spent some sweet coin on a nice brush or a bougie set of pencils. If you love fashion, you probably like spending money on clothes. If you're trying to learn a language, you might splash out on a course (or, if we're back in the nineties, a Rosetta Stone CD).

So it's no wonder, then, that when your focus is your weight, looking thin and fixing yourself, your money flows towards those things.

When I think back to the things I spent money on in my pursuit of thinness ... A few bucks every week on celebrity magazines revealing the secrets of Tyra Banks's meal plan, and selling the promise that it'd get us her body (no mention of wealth, privilege, time or genetics, obvs). Ten dollars on some cellulite cream dubbed 'the next big thing' by a women's talk show host (which, by the way, was so fucking weird. You put it on, sat down and waited for it to get all hot and burny. Look, it promised you'd lose weight sitting on your ass. You can't blame a girl for trying it.)

I used to spend about $50 a month on this slimming tea that you drank morning and night. Annoyingly, this actually did 'work', in that it deflated my belly and made me feel quite light, though that was solely down to the fact it had laxative properties.

Putting aside the fact that I was paying 50 bucks a month to risk public diarrhoea, what all this came down to was a vicious cycle of spending on a problem that simply didn't exist. It was a manufactured problem that conveniently convinced me to pour money into buying a solution.

Diet products do really well at upholding this cycle. They are never going to work long term. But while there's a lot of focus on the health implications of yo-yo dieting and losing weight and gaining it again (and rightly so, it's catastrophic), there's not all that much commentary around how much this costs women in future financial confidence. Not only do we lose money that could've been used elsewhere, we miss out on so much more. We're told our worth lies solely in how we look. It serves the patriarchy well for us to outsource our self-worth to a jeans size or a number of wrinkles, because these standards are keeping us distracted, and keeping us spending.

'You don't look five-star enough'

When I was 21, I went for an interview in London for my first 'proper job'. It was in the marketing department of a five-star hotel, so I slid into my nicest Zara dress, did my hair and off I went. The only problem was that I was absolutely streaming with some sort of flu. My body hurt, I was snotty and congested (think Emily at the benefit in *The Devil Wears Prada*), and the last thing I wanted to do was go to London for a job interview. But such was the competitive state of the job market, I could hardly cancel because I had the sniffles.

Despite my stuffy nose, watery eyes and the threat of a cough creeping up on me for the entire hour, I actually interviewed really well. They seemed to love me, and I had experience working in hotel marketing thanks to a placement I'd done for uni.

I had a hunch I was going to get a second interview, and I was right. Yay, go me! There was just one problem: they didn't like the way I looked. Well, in their words, I didn't look 'five-star' enough.

The horror.

I should probably clarify they didn't say this to me directly. It reached me because an old co-worker of mine worked at this place, and before my second interview, he reluctantly let me know that my physical presentation was the only problem they'd had with me. Some people say he shouldn't have told me, but to be fair, he just wanted to help me out by giving me a nudge to dial up the corporate vibes for the next interview.

I was pretty hurt and angry, but probably not angry enough. This was 2013, and, look, we let a lot of stuff go back then. But how dare they comment on how I looked?!

I turned up to the next interview with a slicked-back bun, a pencil dress and a sassy attitude. I got the job, and then turned them down. Ha! While I wasn't necessarily in tune with how fucked up it was for them to mention my appearance, I did know that I was going to struggle there if appearance 'standards' were so strict that a snotty nose could count against you.

This wasn't the only time in my career that my appearance has been called into question. I was let go from a restaurant job because I didn't look 'polished' enough. I was continually pulled up on being dressed inappropriately at another office job (literally all I was doing was existing in a curvy body, wearing clothing that wasn't any more scandalous than anyone else) and a London recruiter once called to tell me that a prospective employer 'couldn't believe' what I was wearing. I was wearing a white shirt through which you could see a very faint pattern detail of my bra. *gasp!* What's worse was I'd really turned it on for that interview. I thought I looked great. But I was a curvy size 14, my teeth were crooked and I had boobs that instantly sexualised any attempt at corporate dressing that I could afford with my £6-an-hour income.

Much like we were conditioned by the diet industry to spend our money on being as light as possible, we've had decades of further conditioning around the standards we need to meet to be employable, costing us money in both the resources it takes to maintain these standards, and also the money we lose when we can't.

We're paid less, and with that smaller amount of money we need to spend a lot more than a man to remain good enough.

'Are you wearing the—' 'Chanel boots? Yeah, I am.'

The media we were surrounded by growing up also played a part in our fractured relationship with money. From gossip magazines and reality TV to sitcoms and movies, the narratives we marinated in were anything but conducive to women's financial empowerment.

Transformation porn

'Transformation porn' was a hallmark of women's media for much of my adolescence. You know, the stories with the big reveal moment when the woman is finally worthy because she's lost weight or hidden her tummy or had her hair done or fixed her teeth. Watching these shows further solidified my belief that the most critical priority in my life needed to be a thigh gap, and that I was one rebrand away from finally being good enough. Whether it was Trinny and Susannah teaching women how to hide their bellies with waist belts, America's budding Next Top Models in their makeover episode or Andi Sachs in *The Devil Wears Prada* in *that* iconic scene where she gets a makeover from Nigel and stuns the whole of *Runway*, we came of age drooling over transformation porn.

Nothing sets us squealing like the big reveal of a transformation. We thumbed through them in magazines, we dreamed of our own rebrand and any time anything went wrong in our lives or anyone hurt us, what were we encouraged to do? Give ourselves a makeover. Capitalism loves a heartbroken woman with a credit card. We developed an entire culture around reinventing or rebranding ourselves after a breakup, so much so that the concept of reinvention bled into every area of our insecurities.

We get hopped-up on changing ourselves from the outside—and spending money doing it—but we forget that we're still the same person on the inside. We cut our hair, change our clothes, get a manicure, buy a new lipstick, and probably, in more modern times, get Botox or fillers. We do all of this in an attempt to reclaim our identity, to take back some sort of control, to squash down the crushing pain of not being enough.

But no amount of Victoria Beckham bobs, or hair extensions, eye-widening mascaras, plumping lip glosses or sculpting dresses will help us heal that pain, or change the person we are. And the longer we believe that we need to change, the longer we're kept in that cycle.

One rent-controlled apartment on the Upper East Side, please!

Our favourite TV shows were a big part of our generation's coming of age. They gave us an idea of what life would be like in our twenties or thirties, and got us excited for adulthood.

Yet somehow I'm still waiting for my flashy magazine job and gorgeous inner-city apartment that I can comfortably afford along with a thriving social life and a model-worthy wardrobe.

There's a lot to be said about how money is depicted in fictional media. Despite there being entire teams of people hired to work solely on the continuity of the plot and the characters, money somehow slips through the net. I guess to some degree it has to. *Sex and the City* would've hit differently if Carrie's financial behaviour was at all plausible, wouldn't it? What these shows did, though, was give us a false understanding of what it meant to be a grown-up. Of what our 'normal person' salaries could really afford us and the types of lifestyles we could lead.

I don't know about you, but growing up watching shows like *Friends* and *Sex and the City*, I'd admire these characters with jobs writing for a newspaper or working in a restaurant or in fashion and living these comfortable lifestyles filled with shopping sprees, trendy apartments and cocktails. The affordability of these things was seldom mentioned. Again, I understand why to a degree, but it all contributed to our avoidance of the financial side of existing.

What sitcoms do really well is depict a relatable, everyday experience of unremarkable people just going about their lives while simultaneously representing an experience that's, financially, almost utopian. Characters very rarely have money issues, and if they do they're short-lived. There's almost never financial conflict, stress or worry, and rarely any evidence of their financial priorities or how they manage to afford coffee-shop coffee and bills and cocktails and designer footwear. Lifestyles are rarely compromised due to financial constraints. And, perhaps most notably, people from different jobs, backgrounds and levels of privilege can seemingly all exist together with not a sniff of financial incongruence.

There was that one episode of *Friends* where Joey, Rachel and Phoebe (the actor, the waitress and the masseuse) admit to Ross, Monica and Chandler (the palaeontologist, the head chef and the . . . transponster? If you know, you know) that they can't afford to go to a popular concert and that their salary discrepancies have been an issue for a while. But after a brief altercation, the issue of money isn't mentioned again.

There was also that episode of *Sex and the City* where Carrie realises she's a bit of a hot money mess compared to her friends. She wants to buy her apartment but has no savings. The bank calls her an 'undesirable candidate for a loan'. And suddenly she's abundantly aware of how her financial mistakes have set her back over the years. Carrie famously claimed that shopping was her cardio, discovered that she had spent more than $40,000 on shoes and declared that she liked to keep her money where she could see it—hanging in her closet. In fairness, we do get a glimmer of financial stress in this episode, even a whiff of the privilege conversation, as Carrie snaps at Charlotte, who got outright ownership of her Park Avenue apartment as part of her divorce settlement. But the financial conversation is over as quickly as it started. Carrie borrows the money from Charlotte and everything moves on as if nothing ever happened. Carrie doesn't seem to adjust her financial behaviour and continues to live an aspirational lifestyle.

Now, I'm not blaming these shows for our generation's financial woes. Sometimes a bit of incongruence is necessary in order for a story to capture an audience, but I think it's an important reflection when looking at the state of financial literacy and financial engagement among the millennial generation. The messaging we grow up with plays an important role in the way we come to understand the intersection between money and lifestyle, and the implausibility of our favourite characters' financial experiences could've had, to varying degrees, an impact on how we viewed our own finances in early adulthood.

The shopaholic trope

Remember the days when shopping was a legitimate hobby? When women would aspire to have girly days trotting around cities or malls with bags and bags of purchases stacked up on each arm? Going shopping with my friends when I was sixteen was as much about living out my dream of being like Cher from *Clueless* or Rachel from *Friends* as it was about hunting down a new blue mascara (what was I thinking?!).

Relating to the women portraying these financial behaviours only serves to keep us behaving that exact way. It's no wonder that women who grew up in a shopping-obsessed narrative continue to hold the belief that retail therapy is the answer to our problems.

Even if these messages didn't infiltrate your understanding of money all that much, you certainly weren't often seeing women engaging in positive money management.

On the rare occasion that money was mentioned in the TV shows that reigned when we were young—speaking more specifically to the fictional ones—the women we looked up to were generally portrayed as financially reckless at worst, and financially disengaged at best. In *How I Met Your Mother*, Lily Aldrin was portrayed as the shopaholic with secret credit cards, and Barney Stinson fulfilled the role of the admirable wealthy bachelor. Lily was shamed for her splurges, but the price of Barney's life-size storm trooper wasn't ever questioned.

We didn't see women navigating their careers against the gender pay gap, we didn't see anyone budgeting or hear any whisper of a spending plan. We didn't know people's financial priorities, how they afforded their lifestyles (probably because they simply wouldn't have), or what kind of financial help they may or may not have had.

I want these memories to remind you that the stage was never set for us to be Good With Money. If you've spent more of your life wishing for a thigh gap than you have building up a pot of savings, it's absolutely not your fault.

The playground of consumption

One of the biggest challenges facing our generation is the messaging we're constantly surrounded by from the external world. Throughout history there have always been temptations and opportunities to spend money on things we don't need, of course, but over the last decade, a culture of consumption has permeated every aspect of our lives.

We live in a time of immediacy. A thought can be turned into a social media post in seconds. We know exactly where our Uber is at any given time (and we crack the shits if we don't). We see someone using a product and before they've even finished telling us what it is, we can be on the webpage and adding it to our cart.

It's a far cry from the world we grew up in. We would send texts without read receipts, wait until off-peak call times to ring a friend, book a taxi with no idea when it would arrive, wonder how old a celebrity was without immediately googling to find out, or order a pizza with zero ability to track its journey to our house.

Back then, you'd see outfits on TV or in magazines and if you wanted to get them, you'd need to physically find them at a local store. If there wasn't one in your town, or they didn't have it in your size, then no dice—unless you fancied a road trip. Now, we see a photo or video of that outfit online and can order it right to our door with just a few clicks. All before our brains have even registered whether we actually want or need it.

All of this immediacy has made us reliant on having our needs met in an instant. Every answer is just a google away. Anything we want can be ordered in seconds.

Over time, we have become accustomed to this swift transition from wanting to having, and have started to need more and more stimulation. It's like a game of Hungry Hungry Hippos inside our heads, chomp chomp chomping for satisfaction.

It's why we get bored of that dress we couldn't wait to tear open after one wear. It's why we think we need four pairs of almost identical but kinda different boots. It's why we have multiple makeup palettes. It's why we get more excited by the thought of Uber Eats than by the food that actually arrives (more on that later).

We're coasting through our lives on a consumption-fuelled mission for more, more, more. And the external world is giving it to us—for the small price of our financial safety.

Being Good With Money requires us to make positive financial decisions in our everyday lives. Every dollar we spend is a dollar we don't save, every purchase is a choice between having and not having. But in the modern world, our ability to make good decisions is being tested more than ever.

How we buy

If you were sitting at a pub trivia night and one of the questions was 'In what year was the first product bought and sold on the internet?', what would you guess? Well, open up your trivia bucket because I'm about to drop the answer and it's probably a lot earlier than you'd have thought: 1972. (If that question ever comes up at a trivia night and you get it right because you read this book, send me a DM, okay?)

In 1972, a group of students at Stanford University and MIT conducted an online transaction using APRAnet, the very earliest iteration of the internet. The product? A small quantity of weed. (Classic.)

They only used the internet to arrange a meeting place for the transaction, so many argue it wasn't really true e-commerce. That didn't happen until 11 August 1994 in Philadelphia, when a man entered his VISA details on the internet, purchased a CD for USD$12.84 and subsequently received it in the mail. Aside from the Stanford students' weed mission, this was the world's first e-commerce transaction. The following year, Cadabra Inc.—the company we now know as Amazon—launched as an online bookstore, and the world changed forever.

Interestingly, not everybody realised the significance. The *New York Times* ran an article about the Philadelphia CD transaction, titled 'Attention shoppers, the internet is open', but it wasn't front-page news. In fact, it was hidden away several pages into the newspaper, as though it was just another story of a dude geeking out with his mates. Most people thought nothing of it.

That's how I remember much of the conversation about e-commerce and the internet growing up. I can vividly remember hearing someone say, 'They say you're going to be able to buy stuff on the internet. I can't understand why you would? I'd never put my card details into the computer, how ridiculous!'

. . . yet here we are.

Less than 30 years ago, shopping online was something we didn't think we even *wanted*, and now it's part of our everyday existence.

Depending on how old you are, you might have some memory of how things used to be in terms of shopping, consumption and spending. Maybe you remember getting your pay packet from your first job in cash with a handwritten slip of paper, or you remember putting your card details into the internet for the first time (I did it in the mid-2000s, when I ordered a pair of pink flip-flops with campervans on them for Mum's birthday. I was so terrified that I withdrew all the money from the account at the ATM in case hackers somehow got my details and stole my money.)

How rapidly things have changed.

In many ways, the evolution of e-commerce isn't a particularly bad thing. Technology evolves and it puts products and services in the hands of consumers. More companies can reach more customers, and our needs can be met more easily and quickly as systems and services evolve.

But there is a more sinister side to the explosion of e-commerce that I believe impacts our ability to be Good With Money. The widespread commercialisation of just about everything means that the world we live in is peppered with opportunities to hand over our money. We can buy anything, any time, and get it delivered, all without having to leave our homes.

While this is convenient in many ways, think about the fact that at one point in time, our homes were a safe haven from spending opportunities. Now, all of that temptation follows us everywhere we go. We can drop the equivalent of a week's rent scrolling on our phones when we're unable to sleep, make a major purchase while waiting for a train, or get tempted into buying something we didn't know existed five seconds ago with a simple tap on social media. We get effectively no respite from the endless opportunities to spend, and we're able to turn to spending whenever we have the slightest urge. You only have to look at the Covid-19 lockdowns of 2020 and 2021 to see how easy it is to spend money from the comfort of our own homes. In fact, Australia Post's 2021 eCommerce Industry Report found that online spending rose 57 per cent between 2019 and 2020, while research from Monash Business School's Australian Consumer and Retail Studies unit, also from 2021, found that 50 per cent of online shoppers were making more online purchases than pre-pandemic.

The evolution of e-commerce has meant that the friction between us and consumption has been all but eliminated, with just about every facet of the transactional experience optimised to make it easier for us to spend money.

Think about the way we pay for things. In stores we've gone from having to write cheques or withdraw cash, to being able to swipe a card and sign, to being able to use a PIN number, to being able to tap a card, to being able to tap our phones. Online, we've gone from typing in our card details, to having those card details remembered for us, to being able to check out with the double-click of a button or a scan of our faces.

While it's nice to have a seamless experience, all of these 'improvements' to the way we transact make it easier to spend more money. There's a concept in human behaviour called 'the pain of paying' that captures the negative emotions we feel when paying for a product or service. When we're acutely aware of the money we're parting with and we're connected to the fact that we're handing it over, we're less likely to spend. And, so, while we all love to travel light thanks to Apple Pay and Google Pay, these 'upgrades' to our transaction experience actually serve to reduce the pain of paying by creating psychological distance between us and our money. The less in touch we are with the act of handing over money, the more we spend and ding, ding, ding! The less we have available to save.

Buy Now Pay Later

In 2015, Australia's first major Buy Now Pay Later (BNPL) provider created its first retail partnership. We didn't know it at the time, but the way we consumed was about to reach a whole new level of fuckery. You could now buy something that cost $100 in small, regular instalments without taking out a credit card. No credit checks were done and you could sign up in a matter of seconds. What's not to like about that?

Well, a lot. The industry blew up to become multiple different providers offering credit with all the pros of borrowing and none of the cons (or so it seemed). People were lining up to open an account and chucking sneakers, tech and fast fashion hauls in their carts, ready to slice and dice into payments they could actually afford. But BNPL marked a dangerous turning point for consumption.

Now, I know hating BNPL isn't an original idea, but I want to talk about the way BNPL has changed how we behave.

The more widespread BNPL has gotten, the more accustomed to using it, or at least knowing it's an option, we've become. BNPL is incredibly attractive to our brains thanks to anchoring bias. When a price is broken down into four instalments, we risk allowing our brains to anchor to that lower number and draw conclusions on affordability based on that smaller amount, rather than the broader impact of the full price. As a result, we make decisions on bigger purchases as though they're much lower in cost.

Our purchase decisions depend greatly on the perceived value or enjoyment we're getting from a product and the number of obstacles we might need to overcome to acquire it. By conditioning our brains to consider a $100 purchase as though it's actually a $25 purchase, BNPL providers have shifted our decision-making processes.

There is solid proof that BNPL helps us spend more. Retailers actually make more money when they offer BNPL. Read that again: retailers make more money when they offer BNPL. Not only do more people convert—make a purchase—but the average amount they spend is higher too.

This is the biggest reason why I always encourage people to really dig deep when it comes to their use of BNPL. Even if you're paying off all your instalments on time, you might be spending more than you would have if it weren't available.

The multiplatform problem

As the BNPL sector has grown, more and more providers have sprung into the market. Such is the nature of capitalism, I guess. But this is where the issue of BNPL has quantum leaped into dangerous territory. In the absence of a credit check, a customer could conceivably open five or six or seven different BNPL accounts with different providers. A $1,000 limit might sound relatively harmless in isolation, but when multiple accounts land in the hands of one vulnerable consumer, a larger amount of debt can form, and fast.

The debt we accrue through BNPL is arguably much more messy than other forms of debt, like credit cards or personal loans. These platforms don't generally work on a balance accumulation model. Rather, you pay off each item individually on its own repayment schedule, which can get chaotic.

Say you open four BNPL accounts, each with a credit limit of $1,000. Your total debt potential is now $4,000. For each transaction, you make four repayments. If you make four transactions on account one, you've got sixteen repayments to make on that account alone. Make a further two transactions on account two, and there's eight more. Make an additional three transactions on account three, and there's twelve repayments there. And then one final transaction on the fourth account, giving you four more repayments to factor into your mental load. That's forty repayments to be made across ten transactions.

Keeping up to date can create a lot of chaos in your money management system and leave you open to mistakes that could cost you in late payment fees.

Our obsession with NOW

How annoying is it when you tap your card for your morning latte and the little circle loading thing goes round and round and round? Or when you type something into Google and the answer you're looking for doesn't just pop up? Or when you open Instagram and the pictures aren't fully loaded?

Annoying.

But why is it SO frustrating? It's literally only a few seconds! To put it simply, the evolution of technology has primed our brains to want everything right now.

As a generation, we're often poked and prodded with jabs about our short attention spans, our obsession with having everything now, how accustomed we've become to accessing information in a split second and our penchant for instant gratification. But come on, *everything* has been sped up. Can you blame us?! We can see something we want and check out with our face in a handful of seconds without even getting off the couch.

Ever ordered a parcel and immediately clicked the tracking link because even though you know there is precisely zero chance it will say anything other than 'check back later', you still wanna have a little peek juuuuuuust in case the factory is actually fourteen seconds away from your house and your parcel is already moments away? Or paid more for an item because it means you can get it sooner?

Our obsession with now has been thrust upon us from every single direction. It's mobile phones, it's getting the internet wherever we are, it's messaging and social media and next-day delivery and Uber Eats. We can have anything, any time, anywhere. We can know anything, any time, anywhere. And we can tell the world about anything, any time, anywhere. We've come to expect immediacy.

The mass commercialisation of the internet has doubled-down our obsession with now. Being able to buy things online started to close the gap between wanting and owning. Then came social media, which closed the gap between us and people around us. Feedback became instant: likes, follows, reactions, conversations, comments. It was all suddenly right there all the time.

Our obsession with instant gratification comes down to the fact that gaps between different states of being have become narrower and narrower. We've become very uncomfortable with the grey area between wanting and having, between curiosity and certainty.

Technology, the internet, social media, apps, tracking, data, algorithms . . . all of these things have changed the way we consume. And where there's a conversation around consumption, there's *always* a conversation around money.

Money is the undercurrent of all of our habits, routines and behaviours. If we're consuming information differently, it makes sense that we're consuming everything else differently. And that's where things get interesting for our bank balances.

I introduced this discussion of instant gratification by talking about the way our generation is criticised for our love of instantaneousness. Almost as though it all started with us, as though all of these things were created in response to a demand. But when you think about it, it was the opposite. All of these technologies we use every day were created before we even knew they were possible. They changed the way we behave, the way we think, the way we act and what motivates us. And this, of course, came hand-in-hand with commercialisation. Modalities like the internet and social media and data and algorithms were used to sell us more stuff, more often. And because our brains were primed for it, it worked.

We're poked and prodded with the fact we're entitled, lazy and impatient. All because we were unknowingly trained by and for a system that wants us to spend our money.

The rise of social media

Have you ever heard that saying, 'The way you do anything is the way you do everything'? I always think of those words when I consider the impact social media has had on our lives. It's changed the way we communicate, the way we consume media, the way we interact with brands, the way we understand each other's lives, the way we represent ourselves and, of course, the way we spend money. I could write an entire book on social media alone, but I'll spare you and just talk a little about the ways it has complicated our relationship with money.

As humans, we have a tendency to experience feelings of deprivation if we perceive people around us to have something we don't. This concept is known as relative deprivation. Effectively, we compare our lives against reference groups. The closer our lives align to our reference groups, the less deprived we feel. On the other hand, the more we see other people having, experiencing and feeling different things to us, the more we feel deprived of that thing. When you look to our basic human needs, one of our most primal is the need to belong. Being acutely aware of what other people are doing, earning, buying, spending and enjoying can cause us to want to 'follow the pack', both to belong and to relieve our sense of deprivation.

So what does this have to do with social media? Before we began living our lives through little screens, our reference groups would have been people in our local communities, people we worked with, our family and whatever understanding we had of society more broadly. What social media has achieved is giving us access to much wider reference groups. Suddenly, we no longer exist in the silos of our offline lives—we have visibility over what's going on in millions of people's lives every minute of the day. This exposes us to all kinds of things that we don't have, and leads us to manufacture desires for those things based on the feeling of relative deprivation.

Now, I couldn't possibly write a book and not mention the Dyson Airwrap, so here she is, getting a mention in the first few chapters. In my mind, the Dyson Airwrap is a beacon of millennial social media culture. I can almost guarantee you've either got one, you've considered getting one, you desperately want one or you violently despise its very existence. Whatever the case, you're familiar with her work.

When I was considering buying one in 2020, endless social media posts filled my feeds of people gushing about how great it was, sneering about how it was awful and insisting that nobody should buy it, or sharing their tips on how to get the best results with it. Seeing so many people with this extremely expensive product and seeing how many people said they got it as a gift they didn't ask for (seriously? Who is buying you $900 gifts you didn't ask for, because I need to start surrounding myself with people like that?) made me feel like my life was worse for not having it. It felt like everyone had it and I didn't. Of course, I know that's not true, but its presence in the lives of my reference groups made me think it was.

This is where social media 'hype' can get really dangerous. It's gone so far beyond a cult product getting a write-up in a glossy magazine. We're now seeing that product in the hands of people we relate to, which amplifies that desire and feeling of deprivation if we don't have it.

The result? We're either buying to join our reference groups, or we're feeling crap about all the things we notice we're not experiencing that people around us are. And feeling crap almost always leads to less than optimal financial decision-making.

Lifestyle benchmarks

I'll spare you further harping on about how damaging social media comparisons are. I know you know this; I'm not telling you anything new. The point is, the general financial behaviour that people around us engage in creates a benchmark for us. We look to people like us to determine what's acceptable behaviour—financial and otherwise—and copy that in our own decisions. Evolutionarily, we want to belong. We want to fit in. Imagine you're in an unfamiliar place, perhaps a foreign country or culture, or even just doing something you've never done before, like windsurfing for the first time. If you didn't know how to behave, you'd look at what other people were doing and mimic it.

From a survival perspective, this is helpful. We're programmed to join the masses to survive, like following the crowd who are running from a predator. If you slow down and lose the pack, you die.

But now let's think about our financial behaviour. To what extent are we mirroring the norms of others around us, or outsourcing the appropriateness of our financial decisions to what others are doing?

Growing up, I made a lot of my financial decisions in reference to people around me. When I went to university, everyone had an overdraft. It was the done thing at UK universities. Being in your overdraft was kind of seen as a rite of passage.

I somehow didn't get an overdraft until my fourth year. Sure, I had a credit card, two store cards and a firm belief that all that stood between me and self-worth was a £14.99 bottle of cellulite cream ... but an overdraft was where I drew the line. At least to begin with.

When I did get one, I remember the justification I had in my mind was that *everyone else was doing it, so it must be okay*. We're all fucking up our finances, aren't we? Seeing other people making the same mistakes as me only served to keep me burying my head in the sand.

Now, it's not lost on me how ridiculous that sounds as a 32-year-old woman writing about money. But of course hindsight gives you 20:20 vision. Was I consciously standing there in Topshop, about to buy a dress I'd seen on a member of The Saturdays, thinking, 'I'm doing this because everyone else is'? No, of course not. But it all conflates to a lifestyle benchmark that lets dangerous financial behaviour go almost unaddressed.

If I'd been booking private jets or holidays to Dubai or buying labels like Prada or Dior, that would've been such a vast departure from the behaviour of my reference group that it would clearly be problematic. But because I was adhering to the benchmark I'd seen around me, nothing seemed all that wrong with it. Everyone was saying they were shit with money, and everyone would vow to 'stop spending money' after every night out.

And when we combine this with the explosion of social media, we can start to untangle a little bit more about why we are the way we are with money.

At a social level, there's the widening of our reference groups that we've already talked about. Not only does this mean we have even more people to measure our satisfaction and success against, but also that we're adhering to new lifestyle benchmarks with even more hidden nuances.

Scrolling through photo dumps of designer handbags on marble tables next to overpriced glasses of rosé, pairs of Alias Mae sandals placed next to infinity pools and multi-stop Europe trips brings these lifestyle experiences into your frame of reference. You might think, if people like me are going on Europe trips or drinking at those bars or buying that brand, why can't I? Or, maybe it's acceptable for me to do the same?

Social media has left us making decisions about ourselves, our happiness, our worth and our finances based on what others are doing. We're either one-upping each other, mirroring each other or feeling crap about being perceivably inferior. Essentially, the culture of seeing each other's lives has created a bit of a hot shit sandwich.

I know I said I wouldn't bore you with regurgitated commentary about the dangers of social media, but I do want to step through a brief history of Instagram. Whack on your nostalgia goggles, gang, because we're off down memory lane. (No nail art was harmed in the telling of this story.)

Social media advertising

In 2013, in what would become one of the most powerful acquisitions of all time, Facebook acquired Instagram. And the fabric of society caught fire at the edges and has been gradually blazing into oblivion ever since. LOL, no, I'm kidding. Kind of.

In November of that same year, Instagram introduced sponsored posts. Not the kind of sponsored posts that involve a pretty blonde woman holding up a teeth-whitening kit, but the kind where users could pay money to have their posts served to more people. This was the very beginning of Instagram's rebrand as an advertising platform, where individuals and brands could pay to get their content in front of the people they wanted to see it.

For us mere mortals, that didn't mean much. Why would I want to pay for people to see my very haphazard home nail art or the picture of the Baileys cupcake I made perched atop a $7.99 TK Maxx cake stand? Well, I wouldn't.

But if you've got something to sell, the idea of being able to pay to show it to people who would buy it was revolutionary, particularly for small businesses.

At this point, the change was little more than a tech advancement. We were consuming content digitally and advertising followed. Such is modernity.

But by 2015, advertising was no longer a simple act of showing groups of people with common interests products and services they might be interested in. Now, it was personal. Two years after Facebook acquired Instagram, the Facebook Pixel was born, allowing advertisers to track our interests and behaviours online, making messaging more targeted than ever before. This wasn't just advertising; this was different.

Since then, we've become accustomed to ads following us around the internet. We joke about our iPhones listening to us. If we so much as side-eye a new dishwasher, we're bombarded with ads for them and anything related to them. If you engage with a product on social media, you can bet you'll have ads popping up for it everywhere you go.

I once mentioned a luggage brand on my Stories, completely organically, just saying I was interested in buying one of their suitcases. Followers then reported that Instagram had sandwiched an ad for that brand on the end of my Story slides. Intelligent algorithmic word-matching connected the dots between my mention of the brand and the ad campaign the brand was running, and decided to shoot its shot. (Before you ask, no, creators don't get paid when that happens. The money goes straight from the brand to Instagram.)

Studies have estimated that we see anywhere between 6,000 to 10,000 ads every single day. Every move we make is an opportunity to be sold stuff, and it's changing the way we consume.

Influencer culture

It's critical at this point to firstly clarify that I do not have a problem with the concept of monetised social media accounts. I mean, come on, I've dabbled in it myself.

At a foundational level, influencing has signified the decentralisation of advertising channels and the diversion of advertising dollars from corporate-owned magazines and billboards to individuals, including women, BIPOC, people with disabilities and LGBTQI+ people.

Are there responsibilities that could be better upheld? Yes. Are there issues with the sheer volume of money allocated to influencers of certain sizes, abilities and races? Yes. The industry has several significant downsides. But speaking specifically to our consumption habits, as brands stopped seeing creators as a waste of internet space and began utilising them as legitimate marketing channels, our vulnerability to external messaging increased tenfold.

Suddenly, we weren't being marketed to via glossy magazines. We were being sold to by people *just like us*. People we could send real messages to. People who watched the same trashy TV as us. People who we had developed a parasocial relationship with. People we thought we knew.

Influencing began as an aspiration game. Awe-inspiring travel photography and street style–meets–editorial fashion content filled our feeds, as 'normal' people got a peek into glossy lives that were a far cry from their own.

Then came the realness. We began favouring iPhone uploads over professional or filtered photos, opting to peek into more modest existences that weren't as far departed from ours as the aspirational ones. We could relate to these people. We could afford the stuff they were promoting. It was no longer first-class flights and designer bags, it was hauls from stores we could actually shop at. It sold us a new lifestyle we could actually buy into. And so we did.

But whether you enjoy consuming aspirational content or the more relatable stuff, the outcome remains the same: our exposure to everything we can have has spiralled out of control.

Social media consumption

A US study by OnePoll and Point found that 59 per cent of people had been influenced to purchase something from an influencer's post, and 45 per cent reported going into debt to buy something they saw on social media.

We're being sold to all the time, either overtly, through advertising and intelligent algorithms serving us exactly what they know will make us hand over our cash, or covertly, through our visibility over other people's lives.

Our exposure to the endless things we can buy is out of control, and to make matters worse, e-commerce and social media are becoming more and more integrated.

It all began with the swipe-up link that, at first, was mostly innocently used by creators to direct audiences to blogs or vlogs where they could find more content. But before long we were swiping up to shop. Creators or brands would post an image of something, and include a link to swipe up to see the product page and checkout.

On a logistical level, this experience streamlines our purchase decisions by eroding all the barriers that stand between us and adding to cart. Remember that concept of 'pain of paying'? It's a similar experience here. The smoother it is to pay, the more likely we are to do it. On a habitual level, what this culture of social media consumption has done is drastically shorten the distance between seeing something and owning it.

When you combine this shift in consumption processes with all the visceral connection of social media, the trust we put into people we follow, the need to belong, the relative deprivation we experience and the frequency at which we're sold to, it really paints a concerning picture about how much harder it is to hold on to our money in the modern world.

Spending is trending

With social media at the nucleus of so many aspects of our lives, we've become quite a social society. And our social society loves trends.

My research into what makes a trend likened it to a virus. It starts small, where a few people have it, do it, experience it or are seen with it, before it spreads out into the mainstream where it's focal for a period of time, until it either dies out or becomes endemic. Spread and adoption make a trend what it is, and we're actually wired to like trends more as they become more popular.

It's widely documented that social media accelerates the speed at which trends move through the cycles, making staying up to date an expensive feat. Buying into a trend that will become stale within a handful of weeks or months leaves us buying into the next big thing sooner and sooner every time.

Now, of course I'm not saying we need to withdraw completely from trends. There can be great joy in trend participation, and when doing so in the realm of things like fashion, food and music, we're participating in art, in beauty, in talent. It's not necessarily a bad thing. But we need to be literate in the cyclical nature of consumption, and aware of the financial implications of accelerated trends when this runs atop an undercurrent of oversupply, overconsumption and overexposure.

Minimalism

Rooted in living with less, minimalism promises clean, open spaces, simple capsule wardrobes and minimal clutter (both physical and mental). And yet somehow even minimalism—the very act of having less—has been capitalised on.

Capsule wardrobes have floated in and out of vogue for years now. On the off chance you're not familiar, the capsule wardrobe concept is based on having a set number of items in your closet that are strategically chosen to work together. Usually clad with black, white, grey, camel or navy basics, capsule wardrobes aim to create efficiency, versatility and functionality. Done right, a capsule wardrobe can allow you to dress for any occasion without constantly feeling the need to buy new outfits. Seems like a stellar idea.

I think most of us have flirted with the capsule wardrobe idea at one point or another. In fact, I think I spent most of 2015 lusting over Pinterest-worthy flatlays of Breton tees, light-wash denim and camel trench coats that made me feel like maybe my dreams of that put-together Parisian aesthetic would come true. But unfortunately, like most minimalism trends, it soon became an excuse to spend. I've watched countless hours of videos on YouTube to the effect of 'things I'm adding to my capsule wardrobe this year'. I've justified purchases by saying I'm curating a capsule wardrobe. I've culled my entire wardrobe with the intention of 'starting again from scratch', only to realise down the track that the only thing that attracted me to that idea was the bit where I have a decent excuse to go and buy clothing. The bit where I withdraw from filling my cart with sale bargains and buying something I saw on a celebrity? That bit I clearly wasn't so keen on.

The other place minimalism has taken hold is in the home. Appealing images of clutter-free homes continue to adorn the pages of magazines and social feeds, parroting the message of 'live with less'. But what I've found over the years is that to participate in these trends, you often have to buy in. Now, don't get me wrong, it's always been absolutely possible to practise true minimalism. To take the principles of living with less without googling which store stocks the Boucle armchair in the photo. To actually work with what you've got and not stress about what it looks like. But so often we miss the point and end up tumbling into another vortex of spending temptation.

Then there's the trend of organisation porn. Why do I spend hours watching people restock their Audi Q5s to the diddy of ASMR tones, unfurl eighteen different types of ice from moulds shaped like poodles into a freezer drawer seemingly dedicated entirely to ice (how?), and restock their pantries with thousands of dollars' worth of pre-packaged snacks that admittedly do make me feel a smidge less guilty about using Glad Wrap on my half-dead avocado this morning?

Unlike explicit advertising that comes from a brand and actively says BUY THIS THING and shows you how, these trends covertly entice us to buy more and more stuff without saying anything at all. Everything has become an unintentional advertisement. For feelings, for emotions, for status levels, for the next thing we simply can't live without.

I can't say I gave ice trays much thought until I saw this trend. Now I know I can get twenty different types delivered to my door by tomorrow. But should I?

Self-care

Self-care is one of the buzzwords of our generation. It's become commonplace in internet vernacular, synonymous with aesthetic images of bubble baths, candles, fresh flowers and pinot grigio perched atop a marble table. We're encouraged to justify just about anything as an act of self-care, especially when it comes to spending money.

To give you a brief history, self-care was originally a medical term used to describe the practices recommended for those healing from illness or injury. In the 1950s, it expanded beyond the medical field and represented an important practice for activists during the civil rights movement in the US. Leaders of the Black Panther Party employed mindfulness techniques like yoga and meditation during their incarcerations, and later went on to popularise the concept of self-care within Black communities, emphasising the importance of human connection and looking after yourself and your community during a period of potent racial conflict. In fact, a big part of self-care was built upon the idea of establishing medical, social and emotional support for Black communities outside of the institutions that only favoured white people.

When you look at how it began and its original function, it's more than concerning to think of where we are now with the term 'self-care', but it paints an important picture about the power of commercialisation.

We've become so commercialised that we've tumbled into the habit of buying our way through life. Even in the pursuit of self-care, often one of our first thoughts is whether there's any opportunity to buy anything. A cute yoga mat, a meditation class, some expensive yoga pants in which to do said meditation.

There's a lot for us individually to unlearn when it comes to self-care, and while many of the factors that got us here have come from outside of us, we also have a responsibility to ourselves to choose to dismantle these norms.

As I stood in front of my mirror recently, slathering on serum, still a little unsure of whether the moisturiser went on before or after and hoping my Dr Dennis Gross LED mask was charged, I had a thought. Why do I do all this? On the one hand, the soothing luxury spa scent of jojoba was a pleasant experience and I enjoyed that clean, dewy feeling on my skin when I actually bothered with the whole rigmarole. On the other hand, part of me knew that deep down I was doing all of this to slow down the signs of ageing. Did I really enjoy this whole thing? Or was I just doing it to remain as palatable as possible to the patriarchal world for as long as I could?

I guess both were true. But where is the line between maintaining our appearance and doing something that's genuinely for us? What happens when the line is so blurred between what we enjoy and what we've been conditioned to enjoy?

#Selfcare for a price

I've just done a search on TikTok for the hashtag #selfcare. Here's what comes up:

- doing a Ouai body scrub (that costs $67)
- making an iced latte in an aesthetic glass (and here's a link to buy them on Amazon, and, hey, while you're at it, you may as well set up a whole coffee station in your kitchen)

- a multi-step skincare routine that'll cost you $150 a month to maintain
- doing a face mask (not so bad, but some sheet masks cost over $100, yikes)
- shaving your face
- an LED light mask (but only the ones over $600 actually work)
- lighting a candle (okay, more affordable, but the one in the video costs $80)
- a bath with rose petals in it (more budget-friendly, but cleaning those petals afterwards, yeesh!)
- a body care routine (surely we're not doing multi-step body care now too?).

The more we buy into self-care but still don't feel cared for, the more we're going to keep spending and feeling shit—it's a self-fulfilling cycle.

Now it's not lost on me that I'm really pushing the limit with scrutinising trends and the things we spend on. I'm absolutely not suggesting that we stop using that luxurious-smelling serum. Unfortunately, the way we look is a currency in many aspects of life, most notably in the workplace. And we all have bills to pay, after all.

The solution isn't to withdraw from these things altogether. The challenge is differentiating between what we want, and what we've been *conditioned* to want.

We need to have a conversation about how we are conditioned to spend money and explore the power in stepping back, looking at all of this 'stuff' and then deciding, on our terms, the degree to which we want to participate. You don't go to work every day just to have a wardrobe full of clothes you don't wear and a cabinet full of the same serums in different branding. You deserve more for your money than that!

What keeps us spending

One of the biggest roadblocks to being Good With Money is that brands, companies, retailers and marketers know more about our brains than we do. They know how to create desire in consumers, and will spend millions of dollars doing just that, knowing that investment will generate billions in return.

What I hope to do with this part of this book is empower YOU to understand how these tactics work so you can recognise them in real time and stop yourself playing into them if it doesn't suit your financial situation. When we know how our brains work, we can step back from the purchase process and see exactly what's happening. And when we can see why we're about to do what we're about to do, we can intercept the beliefs, thoughts and feelings that lead to us handing over that money, and make more informed decisions on our own terms.

Let's first talk through some of the key tactics used to get us to part with our money.

Selling the lifestyle

If you've ever studied marketing or business, you'll probably have heard of the concept of selling the lifestyle. The crux of it is that you don't sell a product's attributes, you sell the outcome it creates for the consumer. Instead of selling a 600-gram candle with ten hours of burn time, you're selling a moment of calm, peace from the chaos of the day, the feeling of an aesthetic home, or even a personality or identity. Instead of selling an outfit, you're selling a sense of confidence or power, or proximity to the lives of those we aspire to be.

When we're sold a lifestyle, we're buying into something much bigger than the product alone. We can see a future where our life or our identity is enhanced by the product. Selling the lifestyle or selling the experience of a product aims to speak to us on a much deeper level, engaging our emotions and helping guide us through that consideration process. When these emotional appeals collide with the way we feel in the moment, or the ideas we have about our lives or ourselves more broadly, there's a lot more at play than just a transactional exchange of money for product.

Creating 'the gap'

Much of our consumption behaviour is driven by gaps. Gaps between how we feel and how we want to feel, between who we are and who we wish we were, between our current state and the one we aspire to be in. Much like we discussed earlier in the context of diet culture and beauty standards, creating, establishing or widening a gap between who a consumer is and who they want to be opens up a world of possibilities of things you can sell to fill that gap. When brands create gaps in our lifestyles or identities, or widen existing ones, they have the opportunity to position their product as the solution. With this emotional connection, our brains form stories about what purchases can do for us, creating a perfect storm for spending. We'll explore this more in Part 2, where we go deep on our emotionally charged financial behaviour.

Fostering ownership

A popular way brands get us to hand over our money is through perceived ownership. It can be anything from simple things that we've become accustomed to, like slipping on a dress in a fitting room, to advanced technologies, like using augmented reality to see what a lipstick would look like on us, or to place products like furniture into our homes. This all reinforces our ownership bias, also known as the endowment effect. When brands can forge a psychological connection between us and a product by reducing the distance between the two, they offer us a sense of pseudo ownership: we can start to see our lives with the items.

This is where influencer marketing becomes incredibly powerful. Seeing products and services trusted by people we look up to, people we relate to and people we admire, helps with that sense of proximity and ownership. Rather than seeing products in advertisements by the brand, we see them in situ, in the context of real life, in someone's home, or worn throughout a day that has shades of our own lives. It takes us that step further than knowing the product exists, and begins to insert the product into our lives.

Repeated exposure

One of the simpler tactics that keeps us buying is repeated exposure. Earlier we explored repeated exposure in the establishment of trends, and similarly, seeing the same ad or messaging over and over again helps it penetrate. There used to be a 'rule of seven' used in marketing and advertising that said people needed to see something seven times to remember it.

The jury is out on what that number is now, given that we're contending with more and more ads all the time, but the premise remains the same: we need to see things repeatedly in order to notice them.

This is why the process of remarketing and pixel tracking works really well. This is when ads 'follow you' around the internet. It can come through social media platforms or via those ugly banners on the sides of recipe websites. (You know the ones that you exhaust your thumb scrolling through, trying to skip over the story about the author's grandma's lemon tree and just get to the freaking instructions. The reason they tell those stories is so there's more material to smush ads into.)

It's easier than ever to hit those multiple exposures of advertising because of digital opportunities and targeting. Previously, you'd have had to see a billboard or a bus ad or a magazine spread seven times for those messages to start sticking around in your brain. Now, the ads will literally follow you.

This process also plays into our human quirk of confirmation bias. Confirmation bias is a cognitive glitch where our brains will pay more attention to information that supports something we already think or believe. This same bias affects how we consume. Once you've seen something you want to buy, you start noticing things that support your need or desire for that product. When you want a new car, you see that car everywhere. When you want to buy an item of trendy clothing, you'll start to see people wearing that style everywhere, and start perceiving different life experiences as evidence confirming your decision to buy it. This is our confirmation bias at play.

By showing us the same products, services and/or brands over and over again, retailers have the opportunity to get in on our confirmation bias, particularly if there's a seed of desire there for the product or brand we're exposed to. If we think we might want to buy something and then we're faced with several exposures to that brand over the next week, not only are our chances of buying increasing with every exposure, but our brains will be seeking evidence that we should get it, so we're primed to receive these messages.

It's not fate that you keep seeing that bag advertised; it's just remarketing.

Anchoring

Anchoring is a pricing and sales strategy that creates demand for certain products and services by using other products and services to guide our desire.

I once made a video while walking through Zara, filming examples of anchoring in their products. Have you noticed how stores like Zara, H&M and others like them are laid out? Up the front, there is the cream of the crop of what they're selling. The more expensive stuff, the stuff that's more nicely merchandised, styled on slim mannequins. These products plant seeds in your mind of the styles and cuts you like. As you move through the store, similar, but cheaper and often lower-quality products are dotted around. Your mind is guided to these products because they seem like a cheaper way to buy into the experience you had at the front of the store. The product the retailer wants you to buy (the cheaper one) is anchored to the products you see early on in your shopping experience, which manipulate your perception of the lower-priced item.

The concept of anchoring is why 'dupes' are such a big part of the way we buy. Dupes, shorthand for duplicates, refer to cheaper versions of other products. These have become commonplace on social media and blogs over the years. A quick TikTok search for 'dupes' brings up hours and hours of videos of the best dupe products, from perfumes to handbags to beauty products.

Viewing products in this way can tamper with how we assess purchase decisions, thanks to the rule of relativity. A $50 eye cream on its own may need some careful consideration, but a $50 eye cream that's a dupe for a cult $250 eye cream seems far better value.

If you've ever queued at a Mecca store, you'll have experienced the power of anchoring by viewing all the little mini products that they position at grab level while you wait in line for the cashier. When you think about it, it's totally genius. You've just browsed the store and been tempted by full-sized products with full-sized price tags, and probably drawn a line somewhere because sadly there's only so much skincare your money can buy. But then, as if by magic, while you wait, you spot the opportunity to buy into that $70 product for just $27 in mini form! 'Shut up and take my money,' we cry, thinking we've somehow gamed the system. Unfortunately, we're the ones who have been played. Next time you're in Mecca, think of me (and beware of the minis).

Manufactured or inflated scarcity

Ever been browsing online and seen an alert that states that 500 other people are also looking at this item? Or spotted a bright red fire symbol saying, 'Only one seat left at this price!'? Our brains have a natural scarcity bias; we will be more inclined to make a purchase if we believe something is in short supply or hot demand.

These tactics have been around for a long time. But the place where traditional scarcity marketing collides with modern media and consumption patterns is 'drop' culture. Several popular activewear brands have been celebrated for garnering impressive growth and cult customer bases, much of which is driven by manufactured scarcity. Don't get me wrong, scarcity isn't all you need to sell, and I'm not squashing the skill it takes to build a brand people want to buy from. But in terms of customer decision-making, seeing a product in limited drops makes that product more desirable and is likely to increase sales. When a brand gets into a flow of dropping product, that product selling out and filling up an eager waitlist for the next drop, we're putty in its hands.

Products will drop with a handful of days' notice, usually accompanied by the threat that the last drop sold out in a few minutes, or hours at best. Our ability to make mindful decisions here is completely eroded, for a few reasons:

» We can't slow down to decide if we really want the product— it's buy now or miss out.
» The hype, fast pace and high demand can flood our rational brains and cause us to buy without thinking.
» High demand and low supply naturally make us want something more.

» If lots of people want in on the product, it's our natural tendency to follow the pack, perhaps even obtaining status by being one of the lucky few to get our hands on something.

» Short windows of availability leave us with little opportunity to decide whether we can actually afford it.

Novelty

Y'know what humans love? Novelty. I am a sucker for it. And brands know it. When we see something we've not seen before, perhaps a collaboration between two brands, a unique flavour of a product or a special edition colourway, we just can't resist.

Last year I had to talk myself out of buying a special edition bottle of gin that was part of a collaboration between a skincare brand and a distiller. It was labelled in the signature cult colour of the skincare company, but other than that, it was really just . . . plain old gin? And yet I still considered spending $100 to buy it, because it was novel, even though I didn't want to buy gin for any other reason. Thankfully, I stopped myself in my tracks, recognising that the novelty had got me and backing away slowly while I still had my head screwed on.

Our love of novelty also feeds off our love of nostalgia. *Barbie* is proof of how much we love the juxtaposition of our childhood memories playing out in our adult lives.

A quick Google search for the term 'Barbie special edition' the day before the movie was released in Australia brought up endless products that had been shoehorned into the cultural zeitgeist. Here are some of them:

- fluffy EMU slippers in Barbie pink
- Barbie x Fossil watch
- Barbie Dreamhouse Glasshouse candle
- Mermade hair styler: Barbie edition
- Barbie special edition Crocs
- OPI x Barbie nail polish set
- Barbie special edition Polaroid camera.

Seeing the movie with your mates might cost you $30, but participating in the consumption of the *Barbie* moment will cost you a lot more. I'm not saying that buying into the cultural moment is off limits—I'd wear those EMU slippers if I didn't already have a grey pair from a few years back—but we must have an awareness of what's being sold to us in order to make decisions on our terms, so we're not left compromising our financial confidence just to feel part of something.

Sales and discounts

On the one hand: the holy grail. Who doesn't love twenty per cent off sitewide or seeing something you want the night before a mega discount day like Black Friday or Vogue Online Shopping Night?

On the other hand, sales and discounts act as a catalyst for alllllllll of our less favourable financial behaviours. Throw in free shipping and it's a recipe for disaster. We've talked about emotional spending, instant gratification, mindless consumption, all those traps that we so easily tumble into. And when you throw a sale into the mix . . . oh, boy, can you say dumpster fire?

Here's why.

Discounting and special offer periods act as a little power boost to everything already going on in our minds by unlocking another cognitive glitch that impacts our behaviour: loss aversion bias.

As humans, we're naturally very loss-averse. We don't like losing things or missing out on things, and this can manifest as FOMO (Fear Of Missing Out). We do not want to miss out. And when you slap a scarcity banner on something our hungry eyes want, we immediately want it even more.

Sale periods douse us in scarcity in two ways.

1. The discount or promotional period is usually timed.
2. Increased demand/reduced supply during sale periods means things may sell out quicker than usual.

These two key factors throw our emotional brains into a tailspin. Here are some narratives you might be familiar with when it comes to shopping sales:

» Urgency buying: 'I'd better get it now because it'll sell out if it's on sale.'

» Supplementary buying: 'I'll have a look around for other bits to get while they're 25 per cent off.'

» Duplicate buying: 'I may as well get both while they're discounted and I can decide later.' (And then you end up keeping both.)

» Manifestation complex: 'OMG, it's on sale, it's fate!'

» False economies: 'If I'm saving $50 on this, I can get that as well.'

» Misplaced benefit: 'OMG, at 40 per cent off, I'm saving $200!'

On top of all this, the general hype of sales can often mean we go hunting for more stuff purely because the discounts are so great.

I often find this with stores I love but can't often afford to buy full price—I'm looking at you, DISSH and SABA. This giddy feeling of getting something we couldn't previously have bought gives us a high that's almost rebellious, leading us to fill our carts with stuff. When we see that giant discount, we're left feeling victorious. We've beaten the system! We've got $1,000 worth of stuff for $240, and we've got a parcel on the way with several chances at happiness inside. Woo freaking hoo!

But then the parcel arrives, the novelty eventually wears off and we're brought crashing back down to reality. Sigh.

The Diderot Effect and spending runways

Have you ever purchased something and then found yourself in a spiral of spending on other things that are loosely related to that item? Enter: the Diderot Effect. This phenomenon is said to have come from a French philosopher in the 1700s who experienced a 'life upgrade' that began with the purchase of an elegant new robe. Shortly after acquiring the robe, he began to notice that all his other possessions—items he'd previously been satisfied with—seemed threadbare and old in comparison. Suddenly, he was consumed by a desire for more and more things that he'd never wanted before.

The Diderot Effect comes into play when the consumption of one thing leads to a knock-on effect of further consumption. It's particularly potent when upgrading things in your life, from your car to your sofa to the clothing in your wardrobe. We feel compelled to buy other things to support and enhance the lifestyle created by the first thing, and 'keep up' with the new standards to which we're becoming accustomed. These are often things we didn't previously want, need or even consider, but the first purchase planted a seed that grew.

I've experienced the Diderot Effect plenty of times. When I was deeply entrenched in #fitspo culture, my consumption spirals would see me purchasing workout guides (ahem, any BBG girlies reading?!), which turned into workout clothes, which led me to protein powder, which soon became pre-workout powder, extending into maca powder, chia seeds and all kinds of other health-adjacent products. All of a sudden, trying to exist in my body cost me a fortune!

In a less toxic example, buying a print for your wall can suddenly lead to you wanting a new couch, which becomes a new throw and pillows, which becomes a new coffee table. Buying a pair of wide-leg trousers can mean then wanting to get the matching jacket. And that then spells a shift in your style so you want to get the same trousers in another colour. And then suddenly your sneakers don't fit the vibe anymore so you switch those out and thus ensues the meandering cycle of consumption that can lead you down a not-very-financially-savvy path.

I like to call these experiences 'spending runways'. You start with buying one thing, and that leads to another, and another, and another, as though your spending is gaining momentum as it goes. Watching out for these runways in your life can help you intercept patterns of spending and keep your money firmly in your pocket.

Saying no to spending traps

Here are some practical things you can do to start getting more aware of the spending traps that surround you.

Audit your environment

The toughest part about all this temptation is that it's completely enmeshed with our everyday lives and routines. We see ads all day, every day, on our screens, on public transport, in our ears and in our inboxes. We need to increase our resilience to these stimuli, and we'll cover how to do this in Part 3 of this book. For now, though, there's one big thing you can do: audit your environment.

Start noticing how often you see advertising or other temptations, overt or covert, and make some tweaks to the media you're consuming. Mute or unfollow brands that you find convince you to spend money quickly. Unsubscribe to marketing emails that get you every time. More than anything, just be aware of how often these things enter your consciousness uninvited. Protect that mental space of yours!

Try a no-spend challenge or weekend

This isn't an original idea, and the concept of 'no spend' can be quite controversial—we'll talk more about why later. But in the context of building up your advertising literacy and resilience to consumption traps, a no-spend day or weekend can help open your awareness to just how many opportunities there are to spend money, and how quickly you can accidentally hand over an hour's pay without a second thought.

Purchase Pathway Reflection (PPR)

The PPR (invented by moi) is an enlightening little exercise that helps you start connecting the dots on where your purchase decisions might have been hijacked. Choosing three things you've purchased, try tracing back the pathway that led you to hand over your money. It might be direct, like seeing something on social media, swiping up and buying it. Or it might be more indirect, like seeing a trend start to unfold, noticing more and more people wearing it, seeing a version you like, getting an email with a discount code and then purchasing. It might be a spending runway that saw one purchase spiral into several more. Being able to see the pathways that lead you to purchases can help you get better at intercepting that process. We'll talk more about reclaiming your spending decisions in Part 3 of this book, where we put you right back in the driver's seat of your finances once and for all.

There's simply too much to spend money on

If we don't currently have something we want, hundreds of iterations of that thing will be presented to us. If we don't have the money, there are endless platforms that will advance it to us. If we've had a bad day, there are countless ways to try to purchase a better feeling. If we've had a great day, there are plenty of things we can buy to celebrate. If we feel happy and content for a second, don't get too comfortable, because we'll soon see someone on a yacht in Europe so we can remember that our lives suck.

These modern advancements have created a culture of consumption that is quite literally stealing our money from us. Our priorities have been hijacked, our insecurities capitalised on, our wants and needs manipulated ...

Existing in this environment strips us of our power and makes us passive, mindless, disengaged spending machines—it's time to reclaim that power, and that's exactly what we're here to do.

When we learn how to make financial decisions based on the things that matter to us, rather than external factors or traps set by retailers and advertisers, we can make decisions based on what we value and our real financial priorities.

It's not about never ever buying anything ever again.

It's not about never responding to a bit of hype.

It's not about always doing the right thing.

It's about *consciousness*. Waking up to all the traps we're surrounded by, getting more aware of our financial participation, taking an active role in where our money goes and being intentional with our consumption.

The greatest challenge here is the dichotomy of being smart consumers and still consuming. Both things can be true. We can be smart with our money and still have the things we enjoy. I think it *is* possible to participate in certain aspects of consumption without living and dying by the latest bronzer to drop in Mecca.

It's all about getting better at filtering out all of this noise and reclaiming our decision-making muscle, rather than having our decisions and priorities dictated to us.

It takes you getting to know yourself, getting to know the world around you and getting to know money, all on a deeper level than you have before. When you break out of the silo of consumption you've been put into, find autonomy in your financial decisions and understand what matters to you and how to align your money to that, you'll experience a sense of freedom like never before. Think of it like a list at the supermarket. When you're in there full-bellied, with a strategic list of what you need, you're far more likely to leave with the right things. Go in there hungry, riddled with cravings, without a list or a budget, and you'll probably leave with all the wrong things.

The same principle applies here. When you know yourself better and you're engaged with your financial priorities, you can make better decisions about the things you're exposed to. Getting to know yourself is an act of financial empowerment.

As Elle Woods argued in court in *Legally Blonde*, 'Happy people just don't kill their husbands.' While far from a watertight legal argument, Elle was right about one thing: happy people do tend to make better decisions. The happier we are with ourselves, the less susceptible we are to the noise of modern consumption culture.

As we'll go on to learn in future chapters of this book, our emotions run the show a lot of the time, and all too often there's a solution ready and waiting for us to buy right when we're the most vulnerable. The happier we are, the less likely these messages are to get through our mental filters.

It's not lost on me that saying 'Just be happy and you'll buy less stuff' is utterly fucking useless to you. You can't just flip a switch and be immune to all of this. But the point I'm making is this: the more attention we focus on slowing down, getting back to basics, enjoying the smaller moments, the little joys (which are often the free joys, believe it or not), and breaking up with the idea that the feelings we want can be bought, the more money we'll keep in our pockets, and the more opportunities we'll have to live life on our own terms.

Now, it's time to meet yourself.

PART 2

Get out of your own way

In Part 1 we explored the ways we've been conditioned to spend, and how the world we live in makes it really, really hard to be Good With Money. But there's another barrier to our own financial success as well: us.

Money itself doesn't carry any meaning—it's just a currency made of paper or plastic—but we're emotional, irrational beings. Money gets its meaning from the emotional transfer that happens when we interact with it.

Our relationship with money is complicated, and that complexity starts from a very young age. It's estimated that we develop a set of money beliefs by the age of six, and throughout our lives, we experience money in myriad different ways, which completely distort how we behave with it. Plus, we're doing all of this against the backdrop of some pretty messy conditioning, as we explored in Part 1.

If you've ever tried and failed to implement a budgeting system or attempted to manage your money and ended up right back where you started, it's probably because that system relies on you being completely rational and doing only what makes mathematical sense.

Without addressing the 'why' behind your financial challenges, logical solutions will fall flat.

So, in Part 2, we're going to do exactly that: look at the range of different ways our emotions and irrationalities get entangled with our finances, from the way we think and feel about money based on our upbringing, to the way we spend it, save it and manage it (or, in many cases, sabotage it). Understanding how our thoughts and feelings influence our financial behaviour can give reason to why we do the things we do with money. Armed with this insight, we can work on reprogramming our money habits to achieve better outcomes.

Our irrational brains

Here's the thing: our brains actually aren't wired for the appropriate management of money. In fact, our brains aren't wired for most of the things we ask of them.

Does your whole existence make sense now?! Mine does.

We're not wired to hoard resources—like money.

We're not wired to exhaust ourselves for no reason—like exercise.

We're not wired to slow down and make considered decisions—like mindful purchases.

The primitive part of our brain was wired to conserve energy, stay with the pack, be quick to outrun predators and use fuel when we have it: behaviours that keep us alive. Retirement planning wasn't something our distant ancestors concerned themselves with, so when we try to put money away for 30 or 40 years' time, or go for a run and tire ourselves out so we can remain healthy into the future, our evolutionary brains are thinking, 'What the fuck?!' Now, I'm no neuroscientist, so I'm just scratching the surface with this stuff, but it really does demonstrate how our natural human programming gets in the way of our ability to be Good With Money.

Our brains have all kinds of functions, but one particularly important part is the amygdala. When we experience a state of threat, our amygdala is in charge of how we behave—and it'll try and get us to relieve that feeling of vulnerability in any way it knows how.

Another important part of our brains is the prefrontal cortex. This is the part responsible for rational thought, planning ahead, setting goals, and doing the 'right' thing.

When we choose to exhaust ourselves through exercise to benefit our hearts in 30 years, that's our prefrontal cortex. When we stop ourselves drinking five litres of soft drink based on the knowledge that there's a shit ton of sugar in it, that's our prefrontal cortex.

But our prefrontal cortex isn't always online. When our amygdala perceives a threat or a strong emotion, our prefrontal cortex shuts down, leaving our primal, threat-activated and fear-responsive amygdala to drive our behaviour. And its priority is relieving the feelings produced by the threat or emotion.

We might think of the prefrontal cortex as being part of the conscious mind, and the amygdala as part of the subconscious. If we managed our money solely with the prefrontal cortex, we'd be much more able to do the right thing all the time. We'd have the foresight to conserve money for the future. We wouldn't feel an emotional connection to things we don't need. And we'd process financial decisions with good judgement and an awareness of long-term consequences.

But we make the vast majority of our decisions in the subconscious part of our minds—which is why managing money isn't as simple as it should be in theory. We have to take into account our emotions in order to master our money habits and make them stick.

When it comes to optimising our financial behaviour, we can hack our brains by training our prefrontal cortex to stay online for longer when making financial decisions. And we can double down by building an emotional connection to the financial outcomes we're striving for—bringing our subconscious mind into the effort as well. Many of the techniques we'll work on together in this book will help you do exactly that.

Our internal creative director

Our emotional, subconscious brain loves stories. We use stories to process information and make sense of our lives. These stories help us make sense of things we would otherwise struggle to understand, like money. Money is an abstract concept. It has no value unless we use it for something—and that's where our emotions come in.

Our emotions make incredibly talented creative directors. We make up stories about all kinds of things when it comes to money, and these stories then influence our behaviour. We hold stories about what products or experiences represent in our lives, about the meaning of money, about what money is for, about ourselves and our deservingness of money, stories about what it means to have money. Whenever we encounter money, our creative director is always on hand to make sense of that experience in a way we can understand. The problem is, these stories can distort our financial decisions. When we untangle the work of our creative director, we can see our financial behaviour more clearly, question our subconscious beliefs and ultimately dismantle the cycles we've been getting stuck in.

Emotional spending

All too often, 'emotional spending' is a term that is weaponised to keep women locked out of the financial conversation. Where men are taught to take risks and build wealth, women are taught to cut coupons and stay away from emotional spending. But emotional spending is something that kept me stuck for a really long time, and I still find it can be a bit of a contentious topic. So, rather than pin the woes of an entire marginalised gender on emotional spending, I want to discuss it in the context of our creative director.

Our creative director's job is to make up stories to give our experiences meaning. Emotional spending is our creative director making sense of our place in a capitalist world, telling us stories about how things can make us feel, often artificially inflating the value we'll get from something in order to make it mean more.

Think back to the last time you ordered a takeaway meal. If you live in a metro area, you probably had this takeaway delivered. Really think deeply about that experience. How good was the food, really? Was it a bit cold? Did they miss something in your order? Were you, on some level, a little bit disappointed?

Probably. Even if you don't want to admit it right now. And on the off chance the takeaway you've called to mind was *chef's kiss* perfection, I can almost guarantee that that was the exception to the rule.

I once polled my community on social media on this topic. While I'm aware my Instagram poll results aren't exactly census-quality data, they did indicate that we're dissatisfied with our takeaway spending about half the time—and that's looking retrospectively, taking into account the fact we really, *really* don't like to admit we made a bad decision.

Read that again. Half the time. 50 per cent of our takeaway orders don't hit the spot. So why do we keep ordering them? Surely, if we're thinking rationally, having a bad takeaway experience should mean that the next time we consider sacking off our perfectly reasonable leftovers or that risotto we actually love making, we should be able to recall that 64-minute wait and the missing cheeseburger?

But we don't. All it takes is a bad day, or some good news, or some bad news, or a discount code or a suggestion from a partner and your creative director is getting out the storyboards, building a whole narrative around what a takeaway represents. It could be a celebration, or a treat, or relief from something really difficult. Or a solution to a lack of time. Or self-care. Whatever the story, it blows your well-intentioned fish and veggie plans out the water—and boom, you're back on the apps.

This behaviour is a perfect example of our brain's incredible ability to artificially inflate the value we think we're extracting from something. It's all about the *experience* we believe we're getting from a takeaway.

When you come home from a crappy day, all the rational stuff you know to be true about the likely outcome of that takeaway order evaporates from your brain, and is replaced with all those artificial benefits. You're recalling the stories you've got parked in your brain about how ordering a takeaway will make you feel better. Up go your expectations, in go your card details. Ordering the takeaway is what meets the emotional need, so when the food arrives and ends up being soggy and disappointing, it's irrelevant to that emotional part of your brain. The rational part of your brain knows it was a letdown, but because you had that surge of emotion that shut off your prefrontal cortex, your behaviour was influenced by the story, not the fact.

I use takeaway in this example as it's a really simple way of demonstrating how our brains think something is going to be much better than it really is. Of how we can ignore all the things we know to be true about it, and still believe we're going to have our needs met if we just spend a little money.

We do this with all kinds of things. How many times have you bought an item of clothing because you thought it was going to change your life? Or done an online order when you were feeling down? Or bought a notebook as a fresh start or because you thought it was the only way to begin a new habit?

All of these purchases are a result of our creative director building stories around who we are and the things we buy. These stories get activated when we experience certain emotions that shut off the prefrontal cortex, and end up influencing our behaviour.

Stories told by my creative director

» 'I'll just grab these basics and then I'm done for the season!' starring Emma Edwards as the fashion minimalist who will never buy anything again.

- 'I need this notebook so I can start journalling and making to-do lists!' starring Emma Edwards as the mindful journaller who changed her entire personality with one notebook purchase from kikki.K.
- 'If I buy this one serum, my skin will change forever and I'll be a glowy goddess and people won't even recognise me!' starring Emma Edwards, who finally got over her not-pretty-enough complex from high school for the humble price of $49.
- 'OMG, if I buy that shirt, pants and top I'll look like that slim, athletic woman with the opposite body shape to me!' starring Emma Edwards, who got over her body image issues after copying an outfit from someone she deemed more worthy than herself.
- 'I'm going to get this because I've had a hard day and I deserve it!' starring Emma Edwards, whose bad day was resolved by buying eye cream.
- 'I'm going to get this because I've had an amazing day and I deserve it!' starring Emma Edwards as the woman who felt the only way to celebrate herself was to buy stuff.
- 'I'll go to Kmart and buy some home gym equipment and then a new activewear set so I can start on Monday!' starring Emma Edwards as the born-again gym devotee whose lack of workout motivation was entirely solved by the purchase of some weights.
- 'I might be a different person once I've read this book!' starring Emma Edwards, who overcame all her shortcomings by putting a book on her bedside table and never touching it again!
- 'I want to have an aesthetic home, so I'm going to go and attempt to style my entire house with one trip to Target!'

starring Emma Edwards, the woman with no interior design skill whose house no longer looks like a hot mess because she spent $200 on prints that she'll probably never hang.

The five stages of emotional spending

The process of emotional spending is kinda like dating a fuckboy: everything looks great at first, then it all comes crumbling down.

First, attraction. We see something we want to buy. We might be actively looking around at things in a store or online or on someone we see in the street, or we might just be living our lives and get served an ad, or get told about something by a friend or co-worker. The item is in our minds as a possibility. Our creative director enters stage left and starts preparing all kinds of fantasies about this potential purchase.

Next, flirtation. We flirt back and forth. The idea has been planted and all of a sudden, we're acutely aware of all the applications for that purchase in our lives. We start seeing the world through the lens of owning that product, which means we'll become more aware of evidence that suggests we should buy it.

Then, euphoria. We've all heard of dopamine—the feel-good hormone that's released when we anticipate pleasure. Contrary to popular belief, dopamine doesn't peak when we get the thing we want to buy; it peaks right before the purchase, because we're anticipating how great our lives will be once we have it. The dopamine actually comes from the lead-up—which is why we often feel a bit meh after we've purchased, as the dopamine has worn off.

Then comes the doubt. The dopamine wears off, all those fantastical expectations we created in our minds about how great something will be for our lives begin to crumble into a cold, harsh reality that wow, a dress didn't change our entire personality. How can this be?!?!

Finally, if we're following this recipe for falling in and out of lust, comes **truth**. That feeling when you know you've fucked up. Where you're scrambling around, looking for a receipt, googling whether Zara will let you return an item without the tag on. (Spoiler, they absolutely will not.)

You're abundantly aware that you were duped by your own creative director. The dress didn't make you a minimalist with a capsule wardrobe. It didn't make you feel as confident as you thought it would. And it wasn't the last thing you'll buy for a while, like you told yourself it would be.

TASK

Regret analysis

To help you start connecting to this concept of your internal creative director, I want you to try to come up with three purchases that you've regretted. Write down whatever they were, then try to remember the problem you were trying to solve with each purchase, or the threat or emotion you were trying to respond to. Were you acquiring a new emotional state or erasing an existing one? Did you feel a certain type of anxiety, fear or stress?

What stories was your creative director telling you about this purchase? What expectations did you have about its impact on your life?

Now, look at your post-purchase experience. How did you feel afterwards? How do you feel now? Where did your expectations fall short?

Our financial experiences and perspectives

Understanding the way we have experienced money throughout our lives is important in understanding our emotional entanglement with it. Money is directly and indirectly interwoven into the fabric of our upbringing, and our creative director starts forming stories to help us make sense of money from an early age.

One of the most common misconceptions about how our upbringing impacts our finances is the idea that our financial reality defines our lifelong relationship with money. We've all heard those rags-to-riches stories of some entrepreneur who grew up broke and decided he wanted to change his life so he built an app and ate instant noodles under his desk at WeWork for two years and now he's a millionaire.

Of course, sometimes these kinds of things really do happen. But it's not the fact that he grew up broke that defined his future plans—it's the *beliefs* he took from that experience. This distinction is really important. It's not so much *what* you experienced, but *how* you experienced it. Experiencing one thing won't necessarily mean you react the same way as someone else who had the same or a similar experience.

Growing up with a single mum from the age of ten meant that money wasn't exactly in abundance in my childhood. Don't get me wrong, my basic needs were always met: we had a house, I was fed, and I had my school uniform and plenty of other material things. I even had a PlayStation, which we all know is the absolute beacon of material wealth when you're twelve.

But I knew we didn't have *money*. I knew we didn't have much financial security. I knew my mum stressed about money, I knew things like car repairs were a worry. I'd hear about the perils of making mortgage repayments, I'd see the realities of redundancy multiple times throughout my mum's working life, and the catastrophic financial implications of mental health problems and marital breakdown. As a result, I was always so confused as to why I wasn't naturally Good With Money. Why wasn't I one of those people I read about who decided to take control of their money after growing up wanting for it? Why didn't I have the wherewithal to actively decide to experience money differently?

Put simply, it's because the beliefs I took from my experience weren't ones that informed financially smart behaviours. Remember: it's not the reality you experienced, it's how you perceived that reality. Two people can have the exact same financial upbringing, but one goes on to be a savvy saver with a high income and a strategic career plan, while the other goes on to find themselves in credit card debt and unable to come up with the money for an emergency.

Siblings are a perfect example of this. I'm an only child so I don't have a reference point here, but if you do have siblings, ask yourself, are they better or worse with money than you? If you all grew up in the same home, with the same level of financial education (or lack thereof), why do you behave differently with money and have different attitudes to your finances? Because you all perceived your experience differently.

To one person, growing up without the things they want or need can fuel a belief that money is scarce and they need to hold it tightly. As an adult they can go on to avoid debt and hoard savings, maybe even struggling to spend money at all. To another person, that same experience can fuel a belief that money is something that's hard to come by, and once you have it, you have to spend it before it leaves you again. As an adult, that belief can play out in finding it hard to maintain savings, in spending money as soon as it comes in, and in feeling like struggling with money is the norm.

This example can be linked to something called learned helplessness. When we grow up viewing money as something that causes difficulty, we grow up expecting this to be the case, and subconsciously uphold the behaviours that make it so. If you see a parent trying hard to manage money and still struggling, it can foster a belief that no matter how hard you try, nothing will ever be any different. As though there's no point in trying to save because money is difficult and there's nothing you can do about it.

The beliefs we form about money from a young age can strip us of the level of empowerment we need to manage money effectively. If you don't believe something is possible, it's unlikely that you'll succeed at it. Like the old saying goes, whether you believe you can or you believe you can't, you are right.

If you grew up with emotional volatility around money, if you saw money cause arguments or become a constant point of conflict, you may have taken that to mean that money is evil, or bad, or that money and love or safety can't co-exist. As a result you might avoid money in adulthood, and withdraw from engaging with it for fear of it causing conflict in your life too. Other people might have had the same experience and therefore strive to avoid money-related conflict at all costs, but this might manifest as actually hoarding money to protect themselves from ever having to argue about it.

The key point I'm making here is this: forgive yourself. Forgive yourself for how you turned out with money. If you don't consider yourself Good With Money, which I suspect might be the case if you're reading this book, it's not because you're unintelligent or greedy or stupid or lesser than someone else in your family, or a friend or co-worker. There's actually a very reasonable explanation for why you are the way you are, and it all comes down to foundational beliefs that you effectively had no control over.

When it comes to being Good With Money, the key is to understand that the beliefs you hold about money influence your behaviour. When you know what your beliefs are, your behaviour actually makes perfect sense. Your creative director is using these beliefs to make sense of situations and informing the way you behave. The good news is, you have the power to create a different reality for yourself. If your current beliefs are causing you to behave a certain way, you can change those beliefs and make more positive behaviour your new normal. We'll work through this together in Part 3.

Your financial window

Your financial experiences come together to form a broader financial perspective that incorporates your overall outlook on money, life and what's possible. It's sort of like your window to the vastness of financial potential that's out there. The smaller your window, the less you'll believe is possible and the narrower your financial perspective will be. The bigger your window, the more you believe is possible and the broader your financial perspective will be.

A big thing that keeps a lot of us from being Good With Money is that our windows are too small. We simply can't see that there's any other reality out there. Maybe we see a few realities that are slightly different from the one we're living, but not different enough to change anything because we ultimately question . . . well, what's the point? Widening your financial window can help you change your beliefs and behaviours by exposing you to a reality outside of your own, and showing you how different paths can lead to different outcomes.

Realising my financial window wasn't wide enough was an important point in my Good With Money journey. I'd grown up believing that money was difficult, that it would leave as soon as it came, and that just when things started going right something would go wrong. I'd not been exposed to examples of financial resilience, like having savings for when things went wrong, or much financial positivity or abundance. I thought that was normal. I thought that the absolute best of it was having a PlayStation and a new pair of school shoes, and that there wasn't much else I could achieve beyond that. Basically, I learned that money just happened to you. You either had some or you didn't.

When you had it, you could buy things. When you didn't, you would struggle. I didn't feel empowered to create or manage my financial experiences.

I used to find myself getting frustrated and angry at myself when I heard of the smart financial decisions other people made at a young age. One of my friends from high school and I once worked at the same place, and we also each had another job at different cafés in our hometown. I remember her telling me that she had a different bank account for the money from one of the jobs and she didn't touch it, she just let it all build up, out of sight, out of mind. By the time we went off to uni, she had about $6,000 saved up. I, on the other hand, had little to show for my hours spent serving paninis, because I struggled to hold on to money. I was either spending it on lip gloss and a pair of Vans, or I was being the generous one in town at lunchtime, shouting everyone a round of potato wedges.

Later, I read a book where the author hadn't grown up with all that much money and so when they moved out of home, they rented the cheapest place they could find and saved really, really hard for a couple of years. They ended up with enough to put down a deposit on a property or go travelling or start a business.

These stories made me so confused and so deeply regretful. Why didn't I do that? Why couldn't I have just saved all that money from my second job? How different could my life be if I'd done that? Why hadn't I felt inspired or empowered to do it?

Put simply, I didn't know that there was a different financial reality available. To me, money was always something that would be transient, something that would control me, something I'd have to stress over. I didn't realise there were things I could do to control it.

Financial flashpoints

While the foundations of our money beliefs form in our brains by the age of six, we also carry something in our mental library called financial flashpoints. These are the major moments that leave a lasting mark on your financial memory. They can happen at any age, and can include things like divorce, family breakdown, major redundancy, a large windfall, major financial conflict . . . anything significant that happens in your life that directly or indirectly relates to money. Our brains take the experience and make sense of it by creating beliefs that continue to sit in the subconscious and guide our decision-making. That internal creative director we met earlier holds on to these memories and uses them as reference points for the stories it creates. Whenever we experience something that reminds us of that flashpoint (even if it's not exactly the same), our creative director makes sense of it by casting the memory onto the new experience.

A big financial flashpoint for me was my parents' separation. Alongside the traumatic experience of family breakdown, the conflict it carried and the financial vulnerability that comes with a single-parent family, there was another significant memory that defined a lot of my financial behaviour for a long time. I was ten when my parents told me my dad was having an affair with someone from work, and he'd be leaving to be with her. That same weekend, my mum bought me a Babyliss hair crimper, which in 2002 was the absolute bomb. I distinctly remember it took something like fifteen minutes to heat up and had three interchangeable plates for tight, medium and wide waves. It was the tits.

My mum later revealed that she'd bought me that to make me feel better ahead of them telling me they were separating, and in the months following their eventual divorce, she admitted that she spoiled me with stuff to try to make it better. For her, it was some way of controlling the situation while also living up to that lower middle-class rule of 'make it look like everything's great'. We didn't want to look like we were struggling.

What my brain absorbed during this time was that if I was sad, or if something traumatic was happening, spending money and consuming stuff would make me feel better. Of course, a Babyliss hair crimper didn't change the fact my dad was leaving, but my ten-year-old brain felt the buzz of getting something new, and it liked it. Spending money became an easy way for me to alleviate discomfort, and became a pattern of behaviour that my brain knew it could reach for when it was reminded of that experience.

Beliefs inform our behaviours

How do our financial windows and financial flashpoints play into our experiences as adults? Essentially they act as reference points for our behaviour. When we make financial decisions, we're farming all that data from our financial 'factory settings' to decide how to behave in different situations.

You only have to look at sports to see exactly how the same experiences can lead to different outcomes. If you look at two individuals who support two competing teams in a sporting competition, those two individuals will watch the exact same game but walk away with a different understanding of what happened.

Consider the emotional nature of sports fandom, too. A supporter who believes their team is hard done by will see every umpire's call as a stab in the back. A supporter who believes their team is exceptional will see every play as a genius example of skill and tact. A supporter who believes their team always comes in second best and always misses out on the glory will feel deep emotional pain at a result that, for a supporter of the team at the bottom of the table, would've been the absolute jackpot.

The point is, beliefs are what inform our behaviours, and when it comes to money, we have a set of financial beliefs that inform how we behave with our money. These beliefs then form an undercurrent for the way we're living our lives. When that undercurrent meets the external world—the advertising, the social media, the temptation, the hectic nature of daily life—they can collide to create a dumpster fire for our money management.

Beliefs are upheld when evidence supports their truth

When we allow our financial factory settings to run the show, we see things through the lens of our own unique window, and interpret events through the frameworks sparked by our own individual flashpoints. As a result, every experience we have serves to uphold our beliefs further, creating self-perpetuating cycles of behaviour.

If you have a belief that money will always be difficult, you perceive experiences through this lens and make them fit.

An extreme example of this is when someone who isn't from an affluent background suddenly comes into money, like through a lottery win or an extremely high-paying job like professional sportsperson. We've all heard the stats about lottery winners who lose it all, or people who inherit a windfall and end up really unhappy and broke. The data is murky on the actual numbers, but the point is this: it's common for people to squander money that comes to them suddenly or unexpectedly.

While on a rational level, more money solves problems (and when we're talking about basic needs being met, yes, it absolutely does), on an emotional level, our financial factory settings don't know how to process this drastic change in our financial reality. Consequently, we use the information we have available from our mental library to make sense of it.

On a much more relatable level than the lottery, we see this play out with lifestyle creep. Your salary goes up but your financial situation never really changes. Now, there's an element of habit and a mindlessness aspect to lifestyle creep, but there's an emotional component too.

Let's also say you grew up believing that money controlled you. When you gradually start to earn more money, without conscious intervention, your mental library will recalibrate your decision-making and your behaviour—perhaps compelling you to spend more so you end up just as powerless over your money as you were on the lower income—and spit out the exact same reality.

Our financial factory settings are responsible for that brick-wall feeling that we can experience when we're trying to create a new financial reality. We might be adamant that we don't want to be living pay cheque to pay cheque, or that we want to have savings to fall back on so we're not stressed by getting our car serviced. But there is comfort in familiarity. We get used to the struggle. So when we're faced with a decision like, 'Should I spend or save this money?', there can be an element of complacency:

'Hey, I can spend it, I'll get another chance to save money next week . . .' And just like that, our financial factory settings have jumped in and stopped us from engaging in behaviour that could have led to a different outcome.

Every time you go over budget and still manage to avoid outright disaster, you're training your brain to think that you can keep doing that. This was a huge sticking point for me, and it was a bit of a lightbulb moment when I realised that I kept allowing myself to sabotage my attempts at saving and spending mindfully because I always somehow found a way to 'fix' it. I'd take on an extra shift or I'd sell something on Marketplace, and so subconsciously, I was proving to myself that I could spend my money because more would be coming. I'd find it somewhere, even if it meant using a credit card.

While we think that we want more money or we want more savings, and we know that these things would make life easier, what we often don't address is what happens to our identity if our financial reality changes. Sometimes there are benefits to maintaining our financial factory settings: they might mean we don't have to realise our full potential, or risk trying something new and failing, or maybe even finally doing that thing we said we'd do if we had more money. If that thing scares us at all—if it's something like changing careers, moving cities, having children or signing a mortgage—then there's psychological comfort in sabotaging our progress towards that new reality by staying exactly where we are.

> **TASK** ....
>
> ## Understanding the relationship between your beliefs and your behaviour
>
> Getting used to connecting your behaviour with your ingrained beliefs and ways of thinking is an important part of the foundational work of becoming Good With Money—as is being able to give yourself grace for financial mistakes you might have made in the past.
>
> There are a couple of different ways you can explore the connection between your beliefs and your behaviour. In fact, you'll probably have some threads of thought presenting themselves while you read this. You might relate to some of what I've shared about my own trajectory, or you might find yourself realising you experienced or believed the exact opposite.
>
> What matters is seeing a connection between your mind and your actions. Start by thinking about your financial experiences growing up, remembering to focus less on what actually happened and more about how you felt or what you perceived. Centring yourself here is key, because how you process these experiences in your own mind is what counts. It can help to think about the way you saw your parents behave with money, and the way they spoke about it.
>
> Then niche it down. Come to those financial flashpoints, those bigger moments that could have punctuated some of the key points in your relationship with money. What happened? How did you feel? What did it make you think about money? Remember to go gently here. Addressing memories from the past can be an emotional and complex thing to do. *Note: ensure you're in a*

safe space mentally and physically when working through these things, and if you're working with particularly traumatic memories, consider raising this topic with a mental health professional or a trauma-informed financial coach.

Think about your financial window. What did you know about money outside of your experience, if anything? How much control did you feel was available around money?

After jotting all this down, turn to a fresh page and ask yourself: what are some financial behaviours you wish you could change? How does money feel to you as an adult? What's going on when you're spending money, or saving money or trying to improve your financial situation? How do you handle financial adversity? One final task that might also help is to think about your perception of your parents' or caregivers' financial beliefs and behaviours. Financial beliefs and factory settings can be generational, so looking at ways your parents lived out their own factory settings might reveal some clues. In what ways have you rebelled against, or mirrored, the behaviours or thoughts you grew up around?

Jot down these answers too, and now, see if you can draw any links. You might find that your behaviour mirrors or rebels against that of a parent or caregiver. You might notice that you struggle with feeling in control of your money, and link that to a memory about when money wasn't in your control. You might say you wish you were better at holding on to money, and find a link to something you heard a lot as a child.

It's important to know that this isn't something you'll sit down and do once and never have to think about again. Understanding your financial factory settings is a state of awareness that feeds into your overall approach to money, something you keep at the back of your mind and that you train yourself to notice over time. It can also be helpful to keep a money journal, or a list on your notes app, of money thoughts you have throughout the day. It might be a niggling feeling of worry, or a pang of jealousy in seeing someone on holiday while you're stuck at work and left thinking, 'How did they afford that?!'

Turning your attention to the way you think and feel about money in your day-to-day life helps you get off autopilot and draw more connections to the why of your financial behaviour.

The answers to these reflections will start to provide a little bit more understanding about where you've come from with money, and the settings you began with that you've not been giving yourself grace for. Seeing your financial behaviour from this cause-and-effect perspective can help you make sense of why you find it hard to be Good With Money—and self-forgiveness is a really powerful step in moving forward.

Seeing money differently is an important part of becoming Good With Money. Factoring in the relationship between your beliefs and your behaviours, or your mind and your actions, will help you develop financial confidence over time.

Your beliefs can be changed and your financial window can be opened—it just takes time and practice, and we'll work on this in Part 3. Awareness is the first and most important step to changing the way you're financially programmed.

We can change our behaviours by changing our beliefs, and change our beliefs by changing our behaviours.

Our self-worth and identity

Just like our creative director makes meaning out of the things we can buy and what money represents, it also creates stories about who we are as people. We all have a relationship with ourselves and a sense of self-concept. Sometimes it's a really positive one, sometimes it's a really negative one. Often, it'll be a bit of both at the same time. So imagine what happens when the stories we've created about money, and about things we can buy, collide with the stories we've created about ourselves.

Believing we're deserving of money (and what money can provide) is important when it comes to earning money, saving it and managing it effectively. If we don't believe we're worth it, we can subconsciously sabotage our financial opportunities, whether that's in our attempts to save money, or when advocating for our worth at work.

Let's start with your money self-talk and how you see yourself specifically with money. How do you describe yourself with money? It's alarming how many of us are walking around happily wearing the label of 'bad with money', or believing that we're irresponsible, that we just don't get it, that there's something wrong with us for acting in ways that veer outside of the most celebrated financial ideals.

A lot of this comes down to the fact that money has traditionally been so taboo. Lots of us were taught that it's rude to ask how much something cost, or how much someone earns. We're conditioned to keep our financial cards close to our chests, and that means no matter whether we have money, don't have money or have any difficulty with managing money, we have to harbour this big secret that can't be talked about.

This leads to one of the strongest emotions associated with money, especially in women: shame. Women experience a lot of shame around money. It doesn't matter whether we have it or don't have it, spend it or save it, keep it or lose it. The way we interact with money can often be traced back to shame, and that's especially true if we don't feel worthy or deserving of it. And in order to feel deserving of money, we need to have a positive relationship with ourselves.

The way we feel about ourselves and our level of self-confidence and self-esteem drastically contribute to the way we behave around money and the outcomes we create for ourselves. To be Good With Money, we have to feel worthy, which is particularly hard when we are constantly told that we're not.

> TASK
>
> ## Money self-talk
>
> Self-talk can be hard to identify because it can be so deeply ingrained into the way we see ourselves. To start understanding

the way you relate to money, read through these statements and rank the degree to which you agree or disagree with them.

STRONGLY AGREE ●———————————————● **STRONGLY DISAGREE**

- I trust myself to spend money wisely.
- I am good with money.
- I manage money well.
- I am in control of my finances.
- I accept my money mistakes.
- I rarely feel guilty about my finances.
- My money worries are minimal.
- I believe I can improve my financial outcomes.
- I can hold money without feeling the need to spend it.

Seeing these positive statements laid out can help you see where you immediately discount yourself and can prompt the negative alternatives to become clearer in your mind. Remember to go gently on yourself with this task. It's okay to come back to it later if you're not in the headspace to tackle it right now.

Now, let's explore some of the ways a fractured relationship with ourselves can dictate the way we behave with money.

We spend money on trying to be enough

As we discussed in Part 1, we've been conditioned to place our worth on things that have nothing to do with who we are. The way we look, the amount we weigh, our proximity to celebrated standards of beauty, our height, our style, our skin. Having a fractured sense of self can keep us stuck in cycles of spending money on trying to feel like we're good enough.

We spend money to feel in control

Spending money is something we can control, so when we feel out of control, we often seek to reclaim our emotions by spending. If we're feeling bad about ourselves, or we've had a bad day, or we're dealing with an emotion we can't handle, spending is an easy way to feel like things are happening on our terms. This is especially potent when we're feeling like we need to change ourselves, or be like someone else, or fix the myriad problems we believe we have with ourselves—whatever the issue, there's a solution we can purchase.

This same logic can apply when we try to change our financial situation and are hit with an unexpected barrier. Our financial reality feels out of our control, so we revert to the one thing we can control: spending.

We spend money on who we wish we were

As we explored in Part 1, we've been sold the idea that confidence, happiness and enjoyment are on the other end of an online order. When we're unhappy with who we are, we often have a fantasy self who can drive a lot of our financial decisions, and cause us to transfer meaning onto things in order to satisfy our craving to be someone else. Spending money on someone we're not creates a further cycle of disappointment and unmet needs, keeping us rolling the dice for another chance until we find a way to quit believing that the next purchase will be 'the one'.

We financially self-sabotage

Self-sabotage happens when we act in a way that undermines our own best interests. We do it with just about everything in life, from relationships to money to health. Self-sabotage can rear its ugly head when we experience something that feels unfamiliar, threatening or uncomfortable.

Not trusting yourself to hold on to money, or feeling shameful about the fact that you're not a good saver, can cause psychological discomfort when you do try to save. It's your financial comfort zone keeping you safe and keeping you doing what you know, so the second you have the opportunity to save some money and change the situation you so badly want out of, you find other ways to deploy that money, either on something specific, or by allowing it to be absorbed by mindless spending.

We rid ourselves of money

One of the toughest things to grasp when it comes to irrational financial behaviour is our tendency to rid ourselves of money. Consciously, we want to save money. We want to have money, and we want to feel more in control of where our money goes. It sounds totally ridiculous to consider that we're actually deliberately ridding ourselves of money. But trust me, it's a thing.

We can rid ourselves of money in all kinds of ways, from being overly generous with friends and family, to spending it on things we don't really care about that much, to ignoring our finances in order to remove the possibility of our situation being different from what it is now.

Ridding ourselves of money comes back to that lack of trust we have in ourselves to manage our finances. When we don't trust ourselves, or feel like we don't deserve to have money (or the financial confidence it could lead to), or don't believe 'people like us' can have financial stability, it can be far more comfortable to just let go of money.

We bury our heads in the sand

If you've ever ignored your financial situation even though you know it needs attention, I'm right there with you. Avoidant money behaviours are a coping mechanism for the psychological discomfort that comes up when we think about money. We can avoid looking at our bank accounts, avoid making financial decisions, put off paying bills until the last minute (or later!) and spend more money than we want or need to even though rationally we know we'd be better off keeping it for other things.

Avoidance is deeply linked to shame. Not only does it create shame, but it also resolves shame, keeping us stuck in a cycle that compounds. If we feel ashamed at how behind we are with our finances compared to other people we might feel a tension between the need to make some changes and the shame that we risk experiencing if we face the problem. To relieve ourselves of this feeling we avoid it, telling ourselves it'll all be okay or that we'll fix it next month.

That then creates more shame when something alerts us to the fact that avoidance is making the problem worse—perhaps a bill arrives, or we glimpse our overdraft when logging into our banking app to transfer money to a friend—and so we avoid some more.

We fixate on past mistakes

We often allow our past mistakes to define us. Getting hung up on the things we wish we'd done differently can cause us to keep repeating the same cycles—we don't really believe there's any other alternative, so we live up to the limits we place on ourselves.

When these aspects of our self-worth and identity collide with the financial factory settings that we've developed throughout our lives, and our emotional entanglement with money, it makes sense why being Good With Money is a lot more complicated than just crunching numbers.

Our relationship with money

Imagine you were in a relationship with another person, and you were constantly experiencing the things you experience with money:

» noticing the widening gaps between expectation and reality (spending and savings expectations, false promises)

» getting hit with constant, unexpected turbulence (bills, expenses)

» feeling like you're never getting anywhere, just playing out the same old cycles

» and, nevertheless, constantly starting fresh and making new promises

» setting up plans (budgets) and not following through

» avoiding or ignoring one another.

Would you call that a healthy relationship? Well, the same goes for your relationship with money.

When I look back on my life before I started sorting my finances out, the way I was treating money wasn't exactly great.

And the way I felt money was treating me wasn't great either. We were that classic 'on again, off again' couple.

When money would come to me, I'd let it leak out of my life like it was a container of soup in my work bag. I'd speak about money like crap, saying it was hard and difficult. I viewed money negatively and focused on maintaining distance from it. I'd say I wanted it, but then I wouldn't nurture it when I had it. I'd avoid money, both in the sense that I'd distance myself from places it hung out—such as my banking app—and I'd avoid managing it, thinking about it and giving it the attention it needed. Then, when I needed it, I'd blame it for not coming to me.

Had we been on *Love Island*, money would've absolutely ditched me at Casa Amor. And to be honest, I wouldn't have blamed it.

Seeing your money as a partnership can help you connect to your finances in a different way. Relationships are something your brain can actually understand. You can't control what the other person does, but you can control how you contribute to the relationship. And the same goes for money. You can't control everything that happens—we all have different advantages and disadvantages that impact how money plays out for us, from our income level to our degree of privilege—but you can control your own input by cultivating a positive partnership.

> **TASK**
>
> **Explore your relationship with money and how you treat one another**
>
> Have a go at answering these questions about how you relate to and interact with money, and see what you notice about viewing yourself and your money as a partnership.
>
> - How do you treat money?
> - Do you show up for money when it comes to you?
> - How does money support you when it shows up?
> - How do you speak about money?
> - What would money think about you?
> - Do you keep your promises to money?
> - Do you resent money?
> - How do you feel money treats you?

Meeting your inner villains

When your creative director is crafting the stories you tell yourself about money, there's a series of villains they can cast. The role of your villains is to pounce on any opportunity they can find to derail your finances. Meeting, confronting and taming them is an important step in getting Good With Money. And looking at them as identities separate from you can help to release any shame you might be carrying about the fact you've not been Good With Money in the past.

Your villains feed off the narratives that sit in your subconscious, as well as all of the noise from modern consumption and social media culture. When your villains run the show, your financial decisions aren't your own, and they aren't in your best interests.

Here are some common villains who might be stepping in and taking control of your money behaviour.

Change Your Life Charlie

Change Your Life Charlie reckons your best-ever life lies on the other side of your next purchase. Whenever you get an idea in your head about changing a habit or making a positive shift, Charlie pipes up and gets you thinking that you must immediately spend money on stuff to support this big new life change. Charlie acts like they have your best interests at heart—and maybe they're right, maybe a new yoga mat and some activewear *will* help you stick to that yoga goal. But, really, Charlie just wants to keep you stuck.

The tell-tale sign of your inner Charlie is that they often appear immediately following a grand promise. You know the ones. I'm going to run a marathon! I'm going to get fit! I'm going to start journalling! I'm going to learn to cook! I'm going to start making my own clothes!

And no sooner than the words have come out of your mouth, there's Charlie. You're in the Change Your Life Spending danger zone. Suddenly you're attracted to home gym equipment, or new activewear, or alllll the pretty notebooks, or a newfangled kitchen appliance, or some sort of wacky spice collection, or incredible fabrics and patterns even though you haven't sewn since you made a coin purse in Year 8 Textiles.

Makeover Margaret

Makeover Margaret is that villain who has you believing you can outsource your identity and your confidence to the things you buy. They're the one making you think a new outfit or a fancy facial will take away all the things you hate about yourself and finally make you the person you want to be.

Margaret tends to strike when you're feeling crap about yourself, and to take away that feeling, they present you with a raft of shiny products that will solve that problem. Margaret stands firm in the belief that the solution to any of your feelings can be purchased, somewhere, somehow. As a result, Margaret keeps you stuck in a cycle of spending to be someone you're totally not, and treating yourself like crap in the process.

When Margaret's in charge, you'll continually sabotage your financial priorities to roll the dice on the next thing you think will fix your latest hang-up, needing a bigger and bigger hit each time to tame those feelings. This cycle can leave you feeling like your hands are tied when you find things you want to spend money on. It's not even about the stuff; it's about the feeling Makeover Margaret has convinced you you're buying, and the gap you so deeply believe you need to close.

What's The Point Wanda

What's The Point Wanda is spicy. They reckon that, actually, being Good With Money is pointless, and you should just ignore your better judgement and do whatever you want. Wanda's power gets stronger and stronger every time the economic reality for young people is ignored by governments and the media. Wanda feels deeply disenfranchised by the state of the world and your ability to take any control of it.

Wanda will have you spending money on things as a consolation prize for the impacts of the housing crisis, stagnant wages and the fact that the people in charge seem to have absolutely zero regard for the fact the fucking planet is burning.

Wanda is a sneaky villain because, unfortunately, they make some valid points—which makes their influence on your behaviour all the more potent. The planet *is* burning. The housing market *is* cooked . . . overcooked. It's crispy as fuck. And I'm not going to sugar-coat it, getting Good With Money isn't a solve-all for any of that fuckery.

But what Wanda doesn't want us to know is that their voice isn't really serving us. Wanda is actually of service to the oppression of younger generations. Wanda is in bed with the big corporations that profit off our disenfranchisement and disillusionment with our place in the world. When Wanda keeps us spending on stuff we don't really want or need, all because we feel completely forgotten and locked out of life, guess who benefits? The companies selling us the stuff. Okay, sure, we might benefit momentarily too because we've got some shiny new thing, but the long-term benefit doesn't stay with us. It goes to them.

While Wanda might raise some valid points, y'know, like the fact that stopping yourself from placing another online order won't fix the fact that the average house is now ten times the average salary compared to four times the average salary twenty years ago, the solution Wanda's offering you isn't the right one. Taming your inner Wanda might not solve everything, but it puts the power back in your hands.

Keep Up Kara and Comparison Connie

Keep Up Kara and Comparison Connie work as a duo, and when they're at the wheel, they'll have you basing your financial decisions on what everyone else is doing. They'll have you focused on what other people have got and what that means about them and their worth, and convince you that you need to keep up appearances by behaving in the same way.

Whether it's people you know or people you see online, Kara and Connie ensure you're benchmarking what you're doing against your reference groups. As we saw in Part 1, this can send you into spending and consumption spirals in the pursuit of belonging to a group, or even gaining respect from others.

Hamster Wheel Harriet

Hamster Wheel Harriet is that sneaky little villain who convinces you that you can outsource your happiness to things you spend money on. While money can and should be used to make your life enjoyable, where Hazza causes you significant financial distress is when they have you seeking happiness and enjoyment through consumption alone.

The hamster wheel comes into play when Harriet is in the driver's seat of your financial behaviour and suddenly, you find yourself almost unable to stop spending money. Whenever you leave the house, money somehow gets spent, and you realise that most of the joys in your life come with a price tag. You know Harriet's at the wheel when the idea of trying to save money or get Good With Money makes you feel tightly restricted and like you have zero idea what to do with your weekends if you're not spending cash.

Fix It Later Fran

Fix It Later Fran reckons you have the rest of your life to get Good With Money, and doesn't think you should worry your pretty little head over sticking to a budget because future you has it covered. Fran will whisper in your ear every time you try to get on top of your money or start feeling overwhelmed by your budget, and will even show up once you've started making some savings progress. Fran can always find an excuse for you not to sort your money out, and spends a lot of time burying their head in the sand and recommending that you do the same.

Fix It Later Fran has some stuff going on, and they know it. But to deal with that discomfort, they avoid the thoughts and convince you that you're actually fine where you are. Fran loves familiarity, and likes to maintain the status quo to avoid dealing with what could lie on the other side of financial confidence.

Fuck It Fatima

Fuck It Fatima is a curious creature. They always manage to convince you that you'll find a way to deal with the consequences of your actions, so there's no need to worry about what happens if you blow your budget or spend money you don't have.

Fatima likes to convince you to spend money you'd reserved for other things, or use services like BNPL in order to get what you want right now, and then hands over the reins for you to clean up the mess. Fatima is a fan of constantly living beyond your means, mentally spending money before you have it, and borrowing from your next pay cheque with the belief that you'll balance everything out later.

Sabotage Sam

Sabotage Sam likes to pop up when you least expect them. Flaky yet feisty, Sam steps in when you start to make a little bit of progress with your money habits and behaviours, and sabotages the whole thing. They'll read from the script of your negative self-talk and capitalise on any opportunity to convince you you're not worthy, sending you back to where you started like a game of snakes and ladders.

Sabotage Sam can strike if you've put unrealistic expectations onto yourself, or you're trying to rush progress and play catch-up with your finances in order to feel good enough. Sam has no compassion for how hard you're trying, and feeds off of scarcity thinking to send you into a frenzy that gets you nowhere. When Sam is at the wheel, you might find yourself throwing in the towel on your goals, losing focus and motivation with your financial ecosystem, and being compelled to spend any money you've saved in order to feel in control.

Tight-hold Tina

Tight-hold Tina is a little different from our other villains in that they actually don't want you to spend your money—but hold on. All is not what it seems. Tina still doesn't have your best interests at heart.

Tina holds money so tightly that they even struggle to part with it when it serves them. Tina will have you labouring over every single dollar you spend, even if it's going to add value to your life or solve a problem. Even when you have the money set aside for something, Tina can appear out of nowhere and make it really, really hard to part with your cash. Every transaction is painful when Tina's in charge, making money management feel really heavy, restrictive and, ultimately, fruitless. No amount is ever small enough for Tina, and they're always worrying about the next thing that could go wrong.

Tina probably shows up a little less often for those of us reading this book, as they're actually often hanging out with those people who we're told are Good With Money—the ones who save most of their money and won't rest until they've got the best deal on absolutely everything.

But it's important to recognise Tight-hold Tina, because they can actually show up when you start making a bit of progress with savings, and make it really difficult to reap the benefits of starting to become Good With Money.

Your villains all have one thing in common—they want to make money hard for you. While many of them do this by having you spend your money rather than keep it, sometimes your creative director can flip on you and send Tina in to make you feel like you need to hold your money tightly in order to feel safe.

See now why taking control is the number one rule of being Good With Money? With these clowns driving our financial behaviour, we hardly stand a chance!

It's important to understand that we probably have multiple villains at play. And, as we know, we've not only got those villains running the show, we've also got our conditioning from the world around us, and the financial factory settings made in our upbringing to contend with too.

The good news is that in Part 3, we'll dive deep into taking back control, covering everything from learning how to make informed spending decisions, to emotionally connecting to a better financial reality for ourselves.

PART 3

Taking back your power

Now we've looked at the many factors complicating our ability to be Good With Money, it's time to take back control. We're going to confront our conditioning and beliefs, reclaim our decision-making, step off the spending hamster wheel and get into the driver's seat of our finances.

Mastering your money starts with mastering your habits. At first, sticking to good habits can feel like walking a tightrope: needing to watch every step, constantly wobbling and worried you could fall into the abyss at any moment. That's because you're going against your patterns of repetition. But over the next few chapters, I'll teach you techniques for behaviour change that will help you build out your confidence and feel more stable. Over time, as you practise being Good With Money, your positive money habits will start to become second nature.

Getting back in the driver's seat

Being Good With Money is about taking control and getting in the driver's seat of not just your money, but your life.

The first thing we need to do here is to get our feelings and our behaviour to speak to one another. When we *feel* like we're in control of money, we *act* like we're in control of money. To work out what it looks and feels like to be in control of our money, we need to start by looking at our identity.

The identity of being in control of your money

Being Good With Money is a state of mind, a state of being and a sense of confidence. It can mean different things to different people—and it should, because it should feel right to you.

But the vagueness of what it actually means to be Good With Money can make it a little complicated to try to understand what healthy money habits look like for you. It's not as simple as saying, 'Only spend money on this,' or 'Never do this, always do that,' or 'Put this percentage of money here and that percentage of money there.' Sorry, I'm not a big fan of cut-and-dry rules. But there's a lot you can learn about good habits by starting with your identity, and I'm going to use a non-financial example to illustrate this.

Last year, I pretty much gave up drinking alcohol. I do still have a glass or two of nice wine occasionally because I really love good wine; I love the production of it, I love the wineries, I love the foodie culture around it, I love reading *Gourmet Traveller*, I love food and wine pairing—I just love it. The fact it's alcoholic is effectively irrelevant to me. If I could get the same taste in a non-alcoholic wine, I would. But aside from some good faux sparklings, non-alcoholic wine just isn't it.

Anyway, the point is I became a non-drinker.

Stop and have a look at that sentence for a second. What do you notice about the way it's constructed? It's worded using language grounded in identity. It says what I am, not what I do or don't do. The fact I occasionally have a glass of wine doesn't actually change my identity, because I identify as a person who, for the most part, doesn't drink alcohol.

The moment I started identifying as someone who doesn't drink, the habits that were conducive to that identity became abundantly obvious to me. At first, I was finding it easy to avoid alcohol on days when I didn't go to social events, or when I didn't have a bottle of wine in the fridge at home. Then I realised that in order to be someone who didn't drink or who rarely drank, I actually needed to be the type of person who went to dinner and drank a non-alcoholic drink. I needed to go to a wedding and just have lemonade—I needed to be around people drinking and still choose not to drink. I needed to stop assuming I was getting an Uber home and start being the designated driver.

When I started thinking like someone who rarely drank, I gained a lot of clarity around what I actually needed to do.

Now, this example isn't quite the same as money because drinking versus not drinking is much more clear cut. But it illustrates an important point about shifting your mindset to shift your behaviour.

Thinking about the things that someone who's Good With Money does or doesn't do can help you make profound progress in changing your financial habits. Rather than focusing on the money you're spending or what you're saving, you think about the intention and the level of awareness that someone who's Good With Money would have.

Does someone who's Good With Money pull cash out of their savings while in the queue to buy something they saw five seconds ago while battling an icky feeling of resistance because they know it's not in their best interests but they're too fired up to care?

No.

Again, it's not about what they're buying or how much they're spending, it's about challenging the story behind what's happening.

Does someone who's Good With Money decide instead that they're going to set aside $100 a week for the next month so that they can buy the item and therefore 1) ensure the spend is planned for, and 2) give themselves time make sure it's really worth their money rather than acting on impulse? Yes.

Does someone who's Good With Money spend heaps on payday simply because it's payday and the money is there? No.

Does someone who's Good With Money still enjoy payday drinks with their colleagues while knowing that their pay has been spread out evenly across their pay cycle? Yes. (I'll teach you how to do this in Part 4!)

Letting go of the way things were

The hardest part of stepping into a new identity is letting go of the old one we've found comfort in. As we talked about in Part 2, there is comfort in familiarity. And to become Good With Money, there needs to be an element of letting go.

Taking control of where your money goes isn't about restriction, but there will probably be some changes to your spending and consumption patterns, and there can be a bit of resistance here because for so long, you've believed that you're spending your money on things you want, on things that make you happy and on things that give you a certain feeling.

The hardest part here is acknowledging that while, for a short period of time, those things do make us happy, that happiness doesn't last. We're harming ourselves by existing in cycles of consumption that are costing us financial opportunities and emotional liberation.

I rarely believe in tough love, but this is the one instance where I need to be blunt: you can't have both. You can't have the reckless spending and the fuck-it mentality and the YOLO lifestyle *and* enjoy the financial and emotional benefits of being Good With Money.

It's really easy to think we're missing out by changing our money habits. Our immediate focus goes to what we're losing: the stuff we buy often, the experiences, the pseudo freedom we think we feel from being chaotic with our money.

Instead, I encourage you to focus on what you're gaining. What will being Good With Money do for you? What weight will be lifted? What anxieties will quieten down? What opportunities will come to you? Will you be freeing up money for something else you've always wanted to save up for? Will you stress less about unexpected expenses? Will you feel more confident in yourself? Will you break the cycle of constantly clearing out your wardrobe, donating and then buying more stuff? Will you finally be able to do something you've never been in a financial position to do?

As an example, if you're getting fit, focusing on the hour of time you're giving up each day won't be very motivating. But focusing on all the broader benefits you'll get from being fitter and healthier allows you to see the bigger picture.

> **TASK**
>
> ### Letting go
>
> To get ahead of the resistance you might feel when changing your financial behaviour, compile a list of all the ways that getting Good With Money will improve your life. Focus on how becoming Good With Money will add to your life, rather than take things away from it. It's all about big-picture thinking and strengthening your intentionality muscle.

You can spend money on anything you want

Being Good With Money doesn't mean you can't enjoy your life and spend money on nice things. You can spend money on anything you want. *Anything.* The world is your oyster. You just need to do it with two things: awareness and intentionality.

Awareness means visibility over your financial situation; an understanding of how whatever it is you're spending on fits into that situation, what the consequences of the purchase are and what it means for your financial position.

Intentionality means exactly that—doing something with intention. When you spend money intentionally, you're getting your behaviour in line with your values, goals and aspirations. When we spend intentionally we rarely wind up regretting it later. And that's the key difference.

We're not giving up buying things we want; we're giving up buying things we don't. Our money is there for us to enjoy and to use as a resource to support what we want out of life. But we have to get to know ourselves and understand what we value in order to develop a positive relationship with money. Remember, we can have *anything* we want, just not *everything* we want.

I tell you this because there will be resistance. Almost definitely.

The line that separates healthy and unhealthy financial behaviour can actually be quite fine. Two identical experiences can have two entirely different backstories, which is why changing your financial behaviour to get better financial outcomes isn't a simple flip of a switch. It requires reflection, self-trust, experimentation and sometimes even failure—and that's all okay.

Identical behaviours, different backstories

Example: buying a shirt you saw online.

Before you got Good With Money	After you got Good With Money
You're not meant to be spending money because you've decided you need to cut back, but your favourite influencer posts a haul and you click one of the links because the shirt looks so great on them and you wish you could look like that.	You're scrolling social media and you see your favourite influencer sharing a haul and you love one of the items. You notice what it is you like about the item, and think about why it is that you want it. Is this just shiny object syndrome, you ask yourself, or is this something that could actually really add to your wardrobe?
You feel instant shame because you're supposed to be saving money but here you are considering buying this shirt. You try to tell yourself you don't need it but you can't stop thinking about it. You're pulling justifications out of thin air, but the shame is building and you just wish you hadn't seen this top so you wouldn't be tempted to spend.	You think about it for a few days, knowing that if the shirt sells out, it's not the end of the world—if it's really what you want, you can always find something similar. And, after some thought, you decide that it would actually be a really great addition to your wardrobe because it goes with all kinds of things, and it's also made with that fabric you know you love, you know suits you and you know fits well.
You try to stop thinking about it but later that night, you go back onto the site, add the shirt to your cart along with three other things, check out and decide that you'll start your vow of saving again next week.	You've got your splurge savings set aside, and while you were considering spending on some new cleanser, you decide you're going to use up the cleansers you've got and buy the shirt instead.

Before you got Good With Money	After you got Good With Money
Because you've blown your goal out of the water, you end up spending more money than usual over the weekend. You want to get it all out of your system before you start again on Monday.	You order the shirt and decide to pay the $3.95 for delivery instead of buying something else you don't want just to get free shipping, because that would eat further into your savings and that wasn't the plan.

In both scenarios, you're handing over money for a piece of clothing, but in the 'before' scenario, you have little awareness of the financial consequences and very little intentionality. You were stuck in resistance and just wanted to get out. In the 'after' scenario, you're aware of your financial capacity and what the purchase means, and you're intentional in that you're adding something to your wardrobe that you've thought through for more than fifteen seconds. You've not hinged your happiness on being able to have this shirt, and you've neutralised the experience by accepting that if it sells out, something else will come along.

So before we move on, can we mutually agree that from this day forward, you are in control of your money habits? Money no longer controls you. You control it.

Ready?

I simply love this for you.

Getting financially aware

Taking back control of our finances starts with one critical step: getting financially aware. Awareness is the first step in every change, because to put it simply, you can't change a problem you don't know exists.

Getting financially aware is all about deciding to open your eyes to your money. What it's doing, where it's going and what your behavioural patterns with it are. At this stage it doesn't matter what you uncover; all that matters is that you're looking. Looking at where your money is going, looking at your bank balance, looking at your income, looking at how much of your income is being spent on different areas of your life, and looking at your habits, behaviours and emotions.

We're going to start with habits and behaviours, and explore some of the ways you're getting in your own way with money.

A habit is something we do over and over again. It can be positive or negative—it doesn't matter. If we repeat it, it becomes a habit. It's important that we understand that there are habits we might not realise we've built, so that we can break the cycles that keep them going and redirect our behaviour.

We'll first look at this in terms of those classic sabotage behaviours we all know we're guilty of sometimes. Then we're going to get a little bit practical and look at what's going on at the back end—in our bank accounts and transactions.

Behavioural audit

The purpose of a behavioural audit is to establish what habits and patterns are holding you back financially, so that you can devour the guidance in this book with those things in mind. The funny thing about money is that on some level, we know what we need to do. We have an instinct as to what's 'good' financial behaviour and what's 'bad' financial behaviour—the bit we don't know is how to make ourselves behave in a way that's consistent with that knowledge.

Generally speaking, behaviours that aren't conducive to being Good With Money are behaviours that sabotage our financial best interests. I want you to take a look at the Financial Sabotage Bingo Card on the next page and circle the behaviours you identify with.

Did you get BINGO? I certainly would have several years ago, and I still hit the jackpot on some of these to this day. Yes, even me. (We'll talk more about letting go of financial perfectionism in Part 5.)

Now that you've got some visibility over the behaviours that are holding you back, it's time to unpack them. I'm going to talk through some of the key themes involved here to help you get some clarity on what's happening, so that we can work on breaking these cycles and help you achieve financial liberation.

Financial Sabotage Bingo Card

Saying 'Fuck it' and buying something on credit	Pulling money out of your savings to cover an unexpected expense	Pulling money out of your savings for an emotional/impulse purchase
Setting a budget and feeling confident and motivated for a day, before abandoning it	Spending money that could be saved when you feel like your goals in life are too hard to reach	Having a spending blowout after being good for a chunk of time
Going over your budget and then saying 'Fuck it' and carrying on	Mentally spending money before the next payday	Borrowing money from yourself by pulling from your savings and promising to pay it back (but never doing it)
Making ambitious goals and then blowing them	Avoiding looking at your bank account for fear of what you might find	Actively finding ways to spend money on the rare occasion there's some left over
Deciding to save an arbitrary and unrealistically high amount (e.g. $50,000) and throwing in the towel when you don't get there fast enough	Walking out the door and somehow spending $132 without even thinking	Paying a bill or paying off some debt and then immediately thinking about what you can buy to reward yourself for being sensible

Why do we set budgets and not stick to them?

The short answer: because our brains think that setting a plan is what makes the change, and we forget about the fact we have to actually execute that plan. Do you relate?

Don't worry, it's not you. It's actually a very normal human brain blunder. In fact, even those swanky companies that bring in fancy consultants to help them change rarely actually go through with what's recommended. It's the exact same quirk that stops us following through with our budgets.

The long answer: on top of our human tendency to prefer planning change over actually making change, there's that pesky emotional vein running through our finances.

When we sit down and make a budget, we're usually juiced up on artificial motivation—you know, that special kind that only comes when you don't actually have to do anything yet and you're just left alone with your imaginings of how you're suddenly going to transform into a disciplined, rational person when you wake up the next day. God, I hate that kind.

That artificial motivation makes us act from the position of our fantasy self—that's the rational, healthy, money-savvy, exercise-loving, calm, anxiety-free person who only exists tomorrow, and never today. When we're hanging out with our fantasy self, we design a fantasy life. We sit down and we look at what money's coming in, look at what our expenses are (usually missing a few things out), and then make grand plans with whatever's left over.

I have distinct memories of doing this over and over and over again. One memory in particular, I'm sitting on the bed, scribbling down a 'budget' on a notepad, working out how everything will be different with my next payday, how I'll pay myself back for the outfit I just threw on a store card AND manage to save some money by eating tinned spaghetti and only spending $20 on a night out. Next minute: I'm eating a baguette from the uni café and spending double my night-out budget just on pre-drinks. Sigh.

Not only is this financially futile—I mean, nobody ever got financially confident by scrawling down a crisis management plan after a spending blunder, right?—but it's absolute poison for our mindset. This constant state of retrospectively fixing our behaviour with knee-jerk, reactive budgets that set us up to fail can cause us to tailspin into financial anxiety and leave major dents in our relationship with ourselves. It's the same process we go through when we're trying to achieve the unachievable standards we talked about in Part 1.

So there are a number of factors causing us to set a budget and not stick to it. From the budget being completely unrealistic, to directing our energy into the plan and not the follow-through, to the discombobulation that comes with budgeting from a passive 'fix it' mentality rather than an active, intentional, taking-control mentality.

Why do we keep putting money into savings and pulling it back out?

The short answer: because we're setting ourselves up to fail. We're likely saving way too much and not giving ourselves enough permission to be human. A desire to play catch-up can lead to us getting ahead of ourselves, saving money that we actually need for other expenses.

We can also misunderstand our costs of living or the expenses that are built into our lifestyle habits, or be completely disconnected from why we're trying to save money, leaving us vulnerable to emotionally charged behaviour.

The long answer: it can be due to myriad reasons, and often it'll be a few different things at once. Let's unpack some of them in a little more detail.

Emotional problem

One of the top offenders when it comes to pulling money out of our savings is an emotional problem. We're used to dealing with our emotions through spending or consumption, so we pull money out of our savings to treat whatever problem we're experiencing. In this case, it's less about the fact you're pulling money from savings and more about the fact you're engaging in emotionally charged spending—your savings are sort of just the vehicle.

Organisational problem

When we're budgeting and planning incorrectly, we can meet what I call 'budget banana skins'—little slip-ups that derail our progress and throw off our focus, but that could have been fixed with a little tighter planning or organisation.

This often happens when we forget that a friend's birthday is next week and we need to buy a gift. Or perhaps we overlooked the fact that a long weekend is coming up and we have effectively budgeted as though we'll be sitting inside doing nothing when we're inevitably going to be out doing something fun. I'm really playing it fast and loose with the word 'inevitable' there, because let me tell you, me being out and about doing something is rarely an inevitability! But, hey, let's assume you're more interesting than me.

Mathematical problem

Sometimes we're simply miscalculating how much we have available to save, so we put money into savings and have to pull it back out to cover something that was completely non-negotiable. This can happen when we overlook variable costs when calculating our needs versus our wants.

It's fairly intuitive to consider that you need to pay your rent, which is likely a fixed amount each week or month, but you can underestimate or omit completely variable costs like electricity, petrol or groceries.

Prioritisation problem

Sometimes, it's not that deep. (You'll rarely hear me say that, because to me EVERYTHING is that deep. Savour this, it might not come around again for another 100 pages.)

But it's true. Sometimes it's not an emotional thing, it's just that we're having a grand old time spending our money on stuff we love in a totally neutral way. Maybe it's a season of social events or it's that year when everyone turns 30 or gets married or some other sequence of celebrations that has you churning through money like there's no tomorrow. When this is the case, it's usually a prioritisation problem. Sometimes, our savings plans skip over the fact that we need to do some shuffling in our financial schedule to fit life in.

An important part of effective Good With Money management is prioritisation; we simply can't have everything we want all the time.

Focus problem

If pulling money from your savings isn't feeling like an emotional, mathematical, organisational or prioritisation issue, it could be a focus problem. Effective money management requires a sense of focus and direction, and a reason why you're doing this beyond the fact that you just 'should'.

If you're not clear on the reasons you're putting your savings away, you could be lacking focus and therefore compromising on your ability to uphold your desired behaviours. Splitting your savings up into different compartments can often be helpful here, so that you're clearer on what it is that you're pulling money from when you use your savings—will this withdrawal mean you'll have to postpone that holiday by a month? Will it mean you won't be able to afford that hair appointment you've been saving up for? We'll work on this together in Part 4.

Motivation problem

Often our savings success can dry up when we're lacking intrinsic motivation, which is the type of motivation that helps us feel connected to what we're doing, and motivated by the process itself rather than just the external reward. Our motivation might have dried up after having started off really high, or it might never have been there to begin with. Sustaining motivation is an important part of fostering positive financial behaviour, and it directly feeds into a few of the other factors at play. Having strong motivation can act as an antidote to emotional spending patterns, help hone our focus and prompt us to tackle the issue of prioritisation.

The problem with pulling money out of our savings

Pulling money out of savings is one of the greatest demonstrations of how money isn't just mathematical. Let's say by the end of the month, you've saved $100. Here are two ways you could have arrived at that $100.

Scenario A	Scenario B
At the start of the month, you set aside $100 and organise the rest of your money to suit what your month is going to look like. You leave the $100 alone and by the end of the month, you've done exactly what you said you were going to do.	At the start of the month, you get overly ambitious and set aside $300 into your savings. The month gets a bit chaotic and you pull out $50 on four separate occasions. By the end of the month, you've saved $100.
How you feel: in control of your money, like you can replicate this same momentum again next month, and like you're doing what you can to manage your money well with the circumstances you have in front of you.	**How you feel:** like you've stolen from yourself four times, like you can't keep a handle on your money, like you've failed. You might be feeling shameful, regretful, confused, stressed or anxious.

The route you take to your savings balance matters just as much, if not more, than the number in the account. Mathematically, this outcome is the same, but from a financial wellbeing perspective, one option is clearly better. The good feeling you get from scenario A means the stage is set for you to replicate this same behaviour over and over again, enjoying the compounding confidence that comes with following through on your plans for your money, and creating a lifestyle that's conducive to positive financial behaviour *and* the enjoyment of life.

The crappy feeling you get from scenario B is likely to compound into more financial chaos, leaving you lacking confidence in your ability to follow through and stuck in cycles of sabotage behaviours that solve your psychological discomfort at the time but leave you paying for your behaviour, both emotionally and financially, long into the future.

> ### Sometimes *gasp* it's just time to use our savings
>
> Many of us are familiar with using our savings for the wrong thing—you know, pulling money out for all the reasons we've just gone through. But what about when we're using our savings exactly as we should be?
>
> Something I've learned in my years of working in financial behaviour and speaking to my audience on social media is that we *hate* spending our savings. We hate it even if we're natural spenders. We hate it even if we've been saving up for something specific and now it's time to purchase that specific thing. And we hate it even if the savings are specifically reserved to be used in an emergency, and an emergency has arisen.
>
> Many of us go through years of our lives with no financial safety net. No money squirrelled away for a flat tyre or a broken phone. We feel anxious and stressed when these things happen, and we wish we had savings to cover these exact purposes.
>
> Yet if/when we do have emergency savings set aside for that exact purpose, we still hate spending it. And the reason is simple: we haven't emotionally parted with the money.
>
> Setting money aside for things requires us to part with the money emotionally as well as physically. If we're secretly

> including savings in our mental holiday fund, or we're making purchase decisions based on the fact that we can always fall back on that $10,000 we've set aside for emergencies, we haven't emotionally parted with the money.

Why do I set money goals and then throw in the towel?

Another common pillar of financial sabotage is setting money goals and then abandoning the plan in a few days, weeks or months. There can be endless reasons for this, all of which are in some way personal to us. But the key commonality is that our motivation for, or connection to, our goals is waning.

Here are a few explanations as to what might be going on.

» **Success sabotage.** If we're working towards money goals and we start to get close, we can sometimes find this new state somewhat uncomfortable. (Remember how hardwired those financial factory settings can be?) If hitting this new goal would shift our financial comfort zone, we can subconsciously derail our progress so that we can continue in the comfort of the familiar. For example, if you've always wanted to go travelling but have never been able to save up to go, success sabotage might see you spending your travel savings on other things because of a subconscious fear around what it means for you and your identity to be someone who can afford to take time off and explore the world.

- **Disenfranchisement sabotage.** This can happen when our goals are too big for us and we feel too much literal and/or psychological distance between ourselves and the outcome. This is particularly tricky when it comes to saving for huge goals like a home deposit, because the housing market is, well, pretty fucked for our generation. If we're trucking along towards a goal and we're then hit with all kinds of negative news about how house prices have jumped 30 per cent, that disempowerment can cause us to derail our progress to relieve some of the psychological discomfort.

- **Disconnect sabotage.** One of the most frequent blunders I made when trying to get my finances on track over the years was setting arbitrary savings goals based on a number I'd plucked out of my butthole. I'd choose some random number, like $10,000, and decide that saving that much would make me feel like less of a hot shit sandwich, would finally mean I'd 'undone' my financial mistakes, and would therefore mean I was Good With Money. This is a common mistake we make when setting goals—we simply choose to focus on something that relieves our immediate anxiety, without actually thinking through what would improve the situation long term. It's actually an avoidant behaviour that we use to pretend we're taking action. Instead, we need to address what's actually causing the feelings we're experiencing (like our financial behaviour) and look to tackle smaller acts of progress one bit at a time. For example, working on our spending habits and building up $250 of savings, rather than skipping ahead to the $10,000.

Why does one mistake spiral into financial sabotage?

Another fave on the financial sabotage hit list is that classic case of making one mistake and then spiralling into a million more mistakes because you've 'fucked it now'. This was one of my greatest woes. I've been betrayed by my own brain so many times with this cognitive flaw—and interestingly, we do it with just about every act of habit change.

» A day or two off exercise and suddenly we're writing off the whole week.

» A drink during the first week of Dry July and the whole month is ruined so we may as well have another glass of wine (when we wouldn't have had that extra wine if we weren't responding to a sabotage).

» A snoozed alarm and suddenly our new morning routine starts again next week.

» A missed day on our meditation streak and we probably won't see box breathing again for another three to four months.

With money, this can look like making one impulse purchase and deciding that you'll just start again next month. Or running into an unexpected bill and deciding that it means you may as well not bother with this budgeting shit. Or pulling money out of your savings and using that to justify three or four more little 'borrow from myself' moments that you promise you'll pay back on payday . . . but then kinda forget about.

There are a few things that can be going on here to cause this spiralling:

» **Financial perfectionism.** Yep, if you're a perfectionist in other areas of your life, it can translate to your finances too. Don't let perfect be the enemy of progress.

» **A misunderstanding of what it means to be Good With Money.** A mistake doesn't define how good or bad with money you are—it's how you respond to that mistake. Being able to recognise and course-correct is an incredible skill that will serve you far better than pretending you'll never slip up again.

» **Binge behaviour following a period of 'success'.** If a slip-up causes a ripple effect that puts us back where we started (or worse), it can be because the original conditions or standards we set for ourselves were too restrictive or didn't take into consideration our lifestyle, personality or routine.

» **Comfort zone spring-back.** Don't forget: our brains love familiarity. When we set new habits and find them hard to stick to, the first place we want to run back to is exactly what we know, even if what we know isn't comfortable either. There's just something about the status quo.

Your behavioural sabotage audit

You'll intuitively know which of these financial sabotage behaviours apply to you, probably because you'll have been violently nodding your head while reading, or thinking OMG, IT'S ME. Hey, maybe you even took a photo of what you were reading and shared it to your social media and said how much it feels like this book is speaking to your brain . . . ? Maybe. Just saying. Hint hint. Wink wink. No pressure, but I'd love that so much.

What we want to do is note which of these behavioural quirks you relate to so that you can bear them in mind when adopting your new Good With Money ecosystem (which we'll get to in Part 4). Knowing how you operate is one of the BEST ways to build positive money habits, because you can build a system to account for the things you know you find difficult.

> **TASK**
>
> Which of these sabotaging behaviours we've looked at do you recognise in your own relationship with your finances? Write down a few memories of when you've engaged in these behavioural patterns, being specific as to what you'd tried to do, what ended up happening and how you felt afterwards.

Identifying your own behaviour: concentrated periods of focus

We can identify with certain financial behaviours when they're described to us or when someone else admits their money quirks. But it often requires more work to get clear on the cycles of behaviour that actually apply to us.

A great way to do this is through setting up a concentrated period of focus and awareness, by stripping back your spending to the bare bones for a few days or a week.

No-spend challenges are often met with a lot of criticism because of their likeness to fad diets. The thinking here is that when you restrict all your spending, you won't make any lasting financial progress, you'll just end up binge spending afterwards and ultimately end up no better off. For what it's worth, I completely agree. If you're starting a no-spend challenge with the hope of fixing your finances, especially if you're doing so in an attempt to claw back losses after a chaotic spending period, that's what's likely to happen. A more sustainable approach to changing your financial behaviour is likely required.

But that's not to say a no-spend challenge can't be useful as a diagnostic tool. If we strip back our purchases to the bare essentials for one week, with the sole intention of observing our behavioural and habitual impulses, we can learn a significant amount about the way we behave—and use that information to create better habits going forward.

The difference between a productive no-spend challenge and a toxic one is intention. Like a fad diet, a toxic no-spend challenge is one that aims to punish you, to accelerate progress in a short period of time with no real intention for long-term change, or to pursue perfection through a routine that's simply unachievable. Expectations are usually high and motivation starts high too, but tapers off quickly.

A healthy no-spend challenge has a clear and reasonable intention. In this instance, it's to get awareness. Throughout your no-spend week, you might notice how often you go to buy something, you might uncover a habitual spend you'd never clocked before, you might notice how many opportunities there are to spend money in your daily life, you might notice things that trigger you to spend money more than usual. That's all information that can be used to set yourself up for success. The progress itself doesn't happen during the no-spend period; it happens when you implement what you've learned.

Other uses for a healthy no-spend challenge might be to free up some extra money for immediate enjoyment, like the week before a holiday. Before I go away, I cut right back the week before so I can free up that week's spending money for extra fun while I'm away.

> ### My year of buying no clothes
>
> At the end of 2022, I decided that I was going to give up buying clothing for a whole year. At the time of writing this, I'm about eight months in. I've learned so much about my spending habits and it has been such a nice reset. Clothes were always my 'thing', my problem area with spending, and where a lot of my financial sabotage behaviours were directed before I got Good With Money. While I've gotten so much better with spending in general, I still wasn't totally satisfied with the way I was buying clothing. I wasn't spending outside of my means anymore, or constantly pulling money from savings and causing financial chaos, but I just didn't love how clothes made me lose my financial cool. If I did ever make dodgy financial choices, clothes were usually the reason. And so I wanted to take a year to change my relationship with clothing consumption and free up some money in the process.
>
> Some of the most potent things I've learned about my spending habits when it comes to clothing are:
>
> - A lot of my desire to buy clothes actually came from laziness. I simply wasn't bothering to get creative with clothes I already had, or to wear things in new ways. It was easier for me to buy new stuff.
> - Seeing things on social media could transform my state from not even thinking about spending money to mentally spending money very quickly. It's proof that seeing something and being

- able to tap a link and buy it within seconds speeds up our purchase decision-making.
- I'd spent so many years buying clothes to try to be someone I'm not. So far, the no-buy year has really helped me find my own style, find the things I like (and, most importantly, discover why I like them) and focus on feeling good in clothing rather than looking a certain way.
- I buy clothing with grand ideas of the polished cool girl they'll make me, because my brain transfers so much meaning onto the outfits I wear.
- There is so much joy to be had outside of consumption—it just looks a little less shiny when it's not merchandised beautifully or slapped with a twenty per cent off code.
- Learning to say 'No' to these things has been so incredibly powerful. The peace that comes with seeing that temptation rise up and being able to make the decision to walk away has been transformative for the way I view my consumption more broadly.

The key to it all was bearing witness to the things my brain would try to get me to do. It was opening my eyes to the stories I was making up about the things I was buying, and the justifications I would reach for when I wanted to make a purchase.

Let's get practical

Simply being financially aware is more transformative than it sounds. When you choose awareness, your relationship with money automatically improves. Why? Because that switch makes you feel like you control money, not the other way around. While taking responsibility for where your money goes can be confronting, it's also empowering, because it puts the control back in your hands. When you know what's going on, you have the power to make changes. If you don't know what's going on, nothing will ever change.

The CJI framework

Alright, shall we do this? We're going to have a look at your bank statements, or your online banking transaction list, if that's how you roll. Get out your highlighters, or a Word document, or your journal or your spreadsheet, whatever flaps your flares, and let's dive in—and, yes, I've prepared a framework for the occasion. I call it the CJI framework: categorisation, joy, intentionality.

Categorisation

The first thing I want you to do is go through and categorise your transactions. Highlight your essential spends in one colour, and your non-essential spends in another colour. If you're not sure what the transaction is for (happens to the best of us, no judgement), either leave it blank or highlight it another colour.

Some transactions will clearly be essential or non-essential, but others might be harder to categorise. For simplicity, consider your essential expenses the ones you don't actively choose to spend on, and your non-essential expenses the ones you could choose to eliminate. For example, your kid's sports fees might not be literally essential to survival, but they're not something you're going to remove. You can call these essential spends.

Next, review those non-essential spends and break them down further into grouping categories. You can define your own categories, but some popular ones are:

- entertainment
- subscriptions
- education
- clothing
- beauty
- self-care
- sports and activities
- events
- gifts
- dining out and takeaway
- kids' clothing
- kids' toys, games, treats
- alcohol.

Breaking your transactions down into categories gives you a really clear view of where your money is going and where you're indexing highest in expenditure. The good news is, by knowing this stuff you're automatically better with money than you were ten minutes ago—fuck yeah! We love a quick win.

Joy ranking

Now, for all of the non-essential transactions, go through and give each one a ranking out of ten for how much joy it added to your life, or how much value you got from it.

The aim here is to create a heatmap of how much value you're getting out of your money. Lots of low numbers indicate that you're not getting much joy mileage.

I want you to be really critical here. While it might feel like you got a ton of joy from that $70 binge at Cotton On because you're still excited to wear the new stuff for the first time, really think about whether it's true, lasting, value-driven joy, or whether it's just a fleeting splash of dopamine to cheer you up during a stressful period at work.

Intentionality audit

Next, I want you to go through your transactions again and mark each one as intentional or passive. Intentionality is a huge part of being Good With Money, and when we're off our game, often intentionality is what's missing.

An intentional transaction is one you thought through, one you planned, one you haven't regretted or that hasn't compromised your financial position in some way.

A passive transaction is one that just sort of 'happened'. Maybe you went out for a drink after work and then there were more drinks, an Uber home and a Maccas run the next day. It's not that this kind of passive financial behaviour is bad—it'll happen from time to time. But being Good With Money means tipping the scales in favour of intentionality more often.

Review and reflect

This next part is going to be much more self-directed, because it'll depend on what you've found. But I want you to spend some time reviewing and reflecting on your findings.

- Did you notice any patterns?
- What are your highest spending categories?

- What are your lowest spending categories?
- What split of intentional vs unintentional spending did you uncover?
- What did your joy heatmap look like?

Money leaks

Picture this. You run a few errands, catch up with a friend, order some sunglasses off The Iconic. You think, 'Okay, so I spent $27 at the pharmacy, lunch was $40 and the sunglasses were on special for $39, that's like $100 so I should have $200 left,' only to check your bank account and find $47 glaring back at you.

How can this be???

Your first thought might well be: FRAUD. Someone *must* have stolen your card. Then a quick scroll through your transactions slaps you in the face and somehow you're disappointed that your card wasn't cloned. It's worse; you stole from yourself.

(Fun fact, I once rang my bank to tell them I was absolutely 100 per cent certain that someone had spent $74.99 on my card because it categorically was not me. Halfway through my story about how it couldn't have been me because I was home all day sick and didn't spend anything, I remembered I'd ordered a pair of rollerblades online. The horror.)

These dread-inducing experiences are a prime example of money leaks. Money leaks represent areas that money is leaking out of your wallet without you even noticing. Leaks can be small things—think Uber Eats orders or Netflix subscriptions—that add up over long periods of time, or they can be more acute expenses in shorter spaces of time, like stepping out the door on Saturday morning and winding up bankrupt by Sunday night.

Money leaks are a great example of how two behaviours can be mathematically equal but emotionally different. Spending $200 can feel perfectly fine when we've done it intentionally. But when we've leaked $200, it feels awful. We feel cheated, shocked, confused, maybe ashamed. Leaks are almost always a result of a deficit in intentionality and/or awareness, and can be a sign of passive money management: allowing our default settings to run the show.

Money leak litmus test

A simple way to litmus test your money for leaks is to choose a type of expense, estimate either how many times you've spent money on that thing in the past month, or how much you've spent on that category in the past month, and then check your guess against your transactions. If your actual numbers are higher than your estimated numbers, you're leaking money somewhere.

One of the most common leaks I see is supermarket transactions. Often falling under the umbrella of the 'top-up' shop (where you do a regular weekly/fortnightly shop but find yourself popping in for extra things throughout the week), supermarket money leaks can have a drastic impact on your disposable income and your feelings towards money.

I once did a public litmus test on my Instagram Stories asking people to guess how many times they'd visited the supermarket in the past month. Then, to check how many supermarket transactions they had on their bank statement. The results were WILD, with people reporting huge discrepancies between their predicted and actual visits. At the conservative end, some people predicted they went once a week (so four times a month) and

> actually went double the number of times. Others estimated seven visits, accounting for a few top-up shops that they knew they'd done, only to find they'd been 32 times!
>
> Identifying leaks is an easy way to spot behavioural blind spots and unlock extra money in your life. Often these leaks occur when you're engaging in what seems like 'harmless' spending, or in spending you think you've got a handle on. As a result, your guard is down, you're more open to temptation, and half-price Tim Tams are just too hard to say 'No' to!

Spotting money leaks, low-joy spends and unintentional transactions presents an opportunity to make what I call 'low-sacrifice, high-impact savings'. These are things you can cut out of your spending without really noticing any real impact on your lifestyle. These things weren't adding to your life in the first place, so if you can eliminate them from your spending routine, you can free up money without missing out.

When I first started working on being Good With Money, these kinds of questions really opened my eyes. I was surprised at the impact that knowing where my money went had on my financial behaviour, but what shocked me most was how confident I was that I knew exactly where my money was going, when in reality, I didn't.

We all think we're better with money than we actually are. We think we know where every dollar is going, and we think we're able to justify our past financial decisions much better than we really can. Sitting down and getting across our transactions is eye-opening for a reason.

That example we talked about before—estimating how much you've spent and being shocked when your bank balance is much lower—is proof of our ability to overestimate how aware we are of where our money is going. When we exist in the environment we do, with all those pesky opportunities to spend on everything from water to coffee to notepads to those random little knick-knacks at the checkout in Mecca, it's so important that we keep our finger on the pulse of where our money is going.

Confronting your toxic financial beliefs

In order to take back control of our finances, wipe the slate clean and get ready to become Good With Money, we need to confront some of those nasty financial beliefs we talked about in Part 2.

The way we feel about money dictates a lot of our financial behaviour, and understanding how our beliefs play a role in our financial reality is an important step to paving a new path.

When I was unravelling how I managed to make it to 25 with no savings, zero handle on my finances and a feeling that money would never be anything but difficult for me, breaking down the beliefs I had about money started to reveal a lot of answers.

Looking back at how I'd interacted with money throughout my life, I realised I'd always loved having my own money. *Loved* it. Couldn't get enough of it. To me, it was independence. I could do whatever I wanted with it and not answer to anyone. But when I dug into that, I realised that what I loved was *spending* money. Spending money felt powerful, like freedom. Autonomy. Independence. Interestingly, keeping money didn't give me that same sensation. The good feeling I got from having money was only upheld by the possibility of all the things I could use it for in the immediate future. I didn't have that same view of holding money for the long-term future, likely because of my financial window being quite small.

The sense of independence and freedom I got from spending money extended to the way I earned it. I worked in cafés and restaurants from a fairly young age, and the older I got, the more work I could do, picking up extra shifts or taking on side hustles to bring in extra cash. Working backwards, I realised that *earning* money gave me a similar sense of freedom—it was the whole package strung together that sealed the deal. I loved earning my own money, getting paid and then spending it on whatever I wanted.

While I might have been developing a strong work ethic, my commitment to my job only served to fuel my earn-spend-repeat cycle. Whenever I needed more money, I'd just pick up another shift. In my mind, I'd always find a way to make more money, so I had subconscious permission to keep on spending it, because I had proven to myself over and over again that I'd find a way.

Suddenly, my love of spending money (and my apathy towards keeping it) started to make a little more sense. The reason I was the way I was with money was because subconsciously, I believed that it would somehow work out in the end and I'd find the money from somewhere. I'd borrow from myself or I'd use credit or some random luck would come my way or I'd sell something to make up what I'd spent.

I tried this belief on for size by thinking about the times I'd acted against my financial best interests. The time I'd had a crap day and gone into French Connection and dropped $129 on a jumpsuit without much thought. The time I'd bought a Michael Kors bag purely because they were having an incredible sale and

I couldn't say no to the price. The times I'd pull money out of my savings for whatever reason, necessary or not. The belief that the money would always turn up fitted perfectly with my behaviour. That was exactly why I continually sabotaged my financial future, because on some level, I believed I would make it all up later. When I was older, from my next pay cheque, when x, y or z payment came in. I was effectively stuck in a state of living in the future of my finances, spending money I hadn't earned yet, banking on security I hadn't built yet and relying on the possibilities of the future to absolve my anxieties around my wonky finances in the present.

This belief was further upheld by my narrow financial window (which we examined back in Part 2). My conviction that I'd always find a way to make more money was actually rooted in scarcity thinking. I couldn't see that the $100 I was borrowing from myself today wasn't just $100, it was a piece of a puzzle that could add up to something much bigger. That those $100 decisions, if reversed to be saved instead of spent, could allow me to make $1,000 decisions and that there was more that money could offer me. I had no understanding of, or exposure to, what it could look like to experience a level of financial security. My financial experiences had taught me that money would always be hard, and life was about spending it while you had it because it wouldn't be sticking around for long.

As I began to connect the dots between my financial behaviour and my financial beliefs, everything started to make a lot more sense. One thing, however, confused me. One of the hardest pills to swallow when it comes to financial beliefs is that we can hold multiple beliefs at once. I held a belief that money would always be hard, but I also held a belief that said, 'It's only money,' which informed a lot of my 'fuck it' behaviours. I also held the belief that money gave me independence, autonomy and freedom. And that pesky belief that I'd always find a way to make more of it.

When you look at these beliefs individually and then together, some parts of them make sense while others feel incredibly contradictory. On the one hand, money made me feel independent and free; and on the other hand, it was only money. Incongruence in our financial beliefs is quite normal—we're contradictory beings, and multiple things can feel true to us based on different life experiences. But that disconnect between my financial beliefs gave reason to my scatty financial behaviour. Some of my behaviours would honour one belief, other behaviours would honour another, so it's no wonder that I constantly felt duped by my financial outcomes.

Some financial beliefs can be changed fairly quickly—awareness that they exist is often the catalyst for change. Other beliefs take more time and require a gradual shift in order to be phased out.

Rewriting my beliefs began with exploring them and opening my awareness to how they were dictating my behaviour. Then I had to work on deciding what I was going to believe instead. Some beliefs are easier to rewrite than others—some have a clear negative bias that can be challenged, for example, 'money is bad' or 'having money makes me a bad person' or 'money is always going to be hard'. Other beliefs are more difficult. My idea that 'I could always earn more money', for instance, wasn't as easy to counter. There's a fine line between the positive and negative side of this belief. On the one hand, it's a belief that's marinated in avoidance and emotional disconnection. On the other hand, you could see it as abundance thinking, the idea that there's always more money to be earned.

The belief–behaviour continuum

So if our beliefs inform our behaviour, is changing our behaviour all about changing our beliefs? And if we change our beliefs, can we just sit back and enjoy the benefits of our new behaviour without having to do anything? Unfortunately, it's not quite as simple as that. When changing our beliefs, we do have to put in the legwork when it comes to our behaviour too—sorry!

Our beliefs are upheld by the evidence our brains collect to support them. We process information and experiences and organise them to mean something. But if we actively step in and change our financial behaviour to create different outcomes, however unnatural it feels at the time, we can create new experiences that serve to evidence and honour our new beliefs.

I call this interconnectedness the belief–behaviour continuum. Sort of like a back-and-forth communication channel between our minds and our actions that can be tweaked at both ends in order to improve the system as a whole.

Changing our beliefs can change our behaviour, but changing our behaviour can also change our beliefs. This is especially true when it comes to money, because of the inherent link between our financial experiences and our self-esteem. A lot of our money stuff is complicated by the way we feel about ourselves, the confidence we have in our ability to do things and the level of deservingness we feel when it comes to positive financial outcomes.

Changing our behaviour is easier than climbing into our brains and changing our beliefs. If we can step in and deliberately orient our behaviour towards a different outcome, while at the same time offering our brains a new script to read from, we can gradually shift our thoughts, feelings and actions into a place where they all line up and work together.

How to rewrite beliefs and reprogram behaviour

Okay, we've talked a lot about our beliefs, and I know it's a bit of a heavy topic because it's not just something you can click your fingers and change. The good news is that when you work on your finances from a belief *and* behaviour perspective, you're far more likely to have longer-term success, because you're actually reprogramming your brain to see money differently and developing a visceral connection to what you're doing.

Here, I've broken everything we've talked about down into a three-step process to help you with your own money beliefs.

Step 1: awareness
The very first thing we need to do is get aware of our beliefs. These form the script for our behaviours. In order to change our behaviours, we must first change the script. And we can't do this without getting familiar with the current script.

I've got two exercises you can use here to uncover it.

#1: life timeline
Draw a line horizontally through the middle of a piece of paper. Recall as many money-related memories as you can from your life, particularly your early life, and plot them along the line in chronological order from left to right, left being earlier memories, right being more recent memories. Plot positive memories above the

line and negative memories below the line. When you've got ten to fifteen memories plotted out, revisit each one and note down any thoughts, feelings or actions that you associate with that memory. When you're finished, connect each memory with a single line, left to right, tracking above and below the line to capture each memory. What you'll end up with is a sort of line graph of your financial experiences. When you've finished, spend some time looking at this visual representation of your money throughout your life. What do you notice?

#2: then and now
Create two columns on a piece of paper. Label one column *Then* and one column *Now*.

In the Now column (to start with now is slightly easier), list out things you wish you could change about your financial behaviour or your financial reality. Things you wish you did differently, or things you wish you felt differently about.

In the Then column, go back to those money memories. Think about things that you remember your parents saying about money, things you thought about money, the way money was spent or saved, and how it was talked about.

Once you have your two columns filled out, explore each item in the Now column in the context of your memories. What conclusions or links might you be able to draw from these? Extract every potential money belief you can see here into a new list underneath the two columns. Don't labour over right and wrong; just see what connections you can identify. Then, try each of them on for size. See which of them feel right to you when you think about your interactions with and feelings towards your finances.

When I was realising I held a belief that I'd always make more money, I had to try it on for size in the context of the financial behaviours that were holding me back to see if it felt right. You'll know when it fits, because you'll feel a sense of something 'clicking' and your financial behaviour suddenly starting to make sense.

Referring back to your inner villains can be helpful here. Do you see any sign of What's The Point Wanda or Fix It Later Fran? Identifying your inner villains can help you create distance between yourself and your beliefs. The shame that can come with realising we've been operating with irrational beliefs can make it hard to move past them. Realising that I had been harbouring the belief that money would always be there made me feel guilty, silly and shameful that I could've been so naively confident in my ability to fix my own problems despite having zero evidence that I was actually able to do it. Assigning that belief to my villain, in this case Fix It Later Fran, who was sabotaging for me, helped me see it more like training a pet than changing something about myself.

Step 2: rewrite and rewire

Once you're aware of your beliefs and the behaviours they're trickling down into, it's time to rewrite and rewire. Yep, this is the bit where you make that all-important shift in your brain and start building up that Good With Money muscle. Step 2 is all about countering, challenging or shifting your beliefs to serve you better, and then unpacking the behaviours you want to extract from those new beliefs.

To rewrite your beliefs, start by writing down all of the beliefs you identified with in Step 1. List them out one after the other, leaving plenty of room next to them on the paper. Next to each one, challenge the belief with three alternatives.

Here are some example beliefs to help you.

Money will always be hard	• Money can be easy, simple and stress-free
	• Money is simple
	• I am in control of my money
	• I make choices about my money
Money never lasts	• I am capable of holding money
	• I trust myself with money and I manage it strategically for my best interests
	• When I hold on to money, more possibilities and opportunities are available to me
	• I can enjoy my money now while also saving money for my future
I'll always earn more money *This belief is more complex because we don't want to directly flip it to say 'I can't earn more money'—that would be a horrible thing to believe! Instead, we're working on making the belief more conducive to the desired behaviour of saving money. We want to encourage ourselves to keep some of it.	• Money can make my life easier
	• Holding money means feeling secure, calm and at peace
	• I deserve to feel financially confident
	• I trust myself to hold money
	• I don't have to spend money to benefit from it
	• Keeping money brings me possibilities

Wanting money makes me greedy or a bad person	• Money helps me do good things • Money in the hands of people like me is a good thing • I am allowed to pursue the security and choices that money can provide me
Money causes conflict	• Money creates freedom, peace and security • Money helps me do good things • Having and holding money is a positive thing
People like me don't get to have plenty of money	• I deserve to have money because I can do great things with it • I am worthy of having freedom • Money is available to me

From your selection of alternative beliefs, choose the ones that you connect with the most.

On a new sheet of paper, write each new belief down then start exploring the financial behaviours and outcomes that would honour that belief.

Belief: I am worthy of having freedom
Behaviours and outcomes:

›› I have money in my savings for when I need it.
›› I can spend money on myself without guilt, shame or negative consequences.

Belief: I deserve to feel financially confident
Behaviours and outcomes:

- I don't make impulse purchases; I make mindful spending decisions.
- I don't pull money out of my savings account; I honour my promises to myself.
- I don't berate myself at the end of the month.
- I follow through on my budget.
- I give myself permission to enjoy some of my money, while knowing that my bills are paid and my needs are met.
- I have savings available to seize opportunities.

Belief: I am in control of my money
Behaviours and outcomes:

- I know where my money is going and why.
- I am strategic with my money.
- I plan ahead and don't make impulsive decisions that I later regret.
- I know my financial priorities.
- I understand how to make money work for me.
- I make positive financial decisions.
- I am building savings confidently.

Belief: I trust myself with money and I manage it strategically for my best interests
Behaviours and outcomes:

- I know what is worth my money and what isn't.
- I am intentional with my spending and saving.

» I set and stick to a budget and it feels easy and in flow.
» I review where my money has gone and make tweaks when things slip out of balance.

Belief: money helps me do good things
Behaviours and outcomes:

» I have enough money to help others when they need me.
» I can allocate my money to things I care about.
» I can make a difference with my money.
» I have savings available to seize opportunities.

These new beliefs and associated behaviours become the new script for you. This replaces the old script and changes the way you behave, act, think and feel. It takes time before this script becomes second nature, and you have to rehearse before you can feel confident in doing it. But you learn by doing, and your beliefs and behaviours change as you experience different outcomes: rehearsing the new script helps you make the changes you need.

Every time we make a decision that honours the new belief and creates a new outcome, it acts as evidence that the new belief is true for us. The concept of neuroplasticity—our brain's ability to change and adapt based on experience—is what makes this true. When we experience new things and deliberately engage with new beliefs and challenge existing ones, we can unlock new pathways in our brains that help these beliefs and behaviours stick.

Step 3: deploy
Step 3 is deployment of your new script in your everyday life. This is where you really reprogram your brain to help you behave differently with your money. You start to create lasting evidence

that you can do things differently and honour and uphold your new beliefs by seeing them play out in reality.

I'm not going to sugar-coat it: this part is the hardest part. It's when you have to actually start making the changes you want to experience in your life. Changing your beliefs and behaviours isn't a one and done situation (I really wish it was!). But, when you make these changes from a beliefs perspective, with that awareness of the beliefs you've been holding and that understanding of why you're behaving the way you are, the changes you create are lasting changes.

You might be thinking, umm, Emma, how exactly do I make these changes, though? I'm reading this book because I feel like I'm not Good With Money, I've started to see how my beliefs are screwing up my behaviour, but where do I actually go from here?

I totally get it.

When we've dismantled our old beliefs, there can be some question marks around the practicalities of actually making the changes, especially if we haven't successfully managed our money in the past. Don't worry; all those gaps on the practical side of money management and advice on how to create a system that helps us keep on top of our money and honour all those juicy new beliefs we're working on wiring into our brains will be filled in Part 4.

Before that, though, I want to quickly look at ways we can explore how our beliefs present in the context of certain behaviours. Sometimes our beliefs can take on new, more targeted forms in certain behavioural contexts. To understand how these present, we can use the ABC model developed by the psychologist Albert Ellis.

ABC model

This is how the model works:

A = Activating event
B = Belief
C = Consequence

You have an activating event and a consequence, and a belief that sits in the middle. The activating event can be a feeling, something that's happened, a behaviour you've engaged in, or something that prompts you to want to spend money. Your consequence might be a resulting feeling, emotion or behaviour, like shame or guilt, that spurs you into a behaviour like spending or pulling money out of your savings.

Your belief is what sits in the middle of those two things and means that the consequence makes perfect sense. Here are a few examples.

Activating event	Belief	Consequence
Had a bad day at work	Ordering stuff online will make me feel better	Spend money online and feel shameful and guilty
Pulled money out of my savings	I'll never get on top of my money, I'm going to be stuck forever	Feel ashamed, helpless, unworthy, don't trust myself with money, vow to do better next time and feel immense pressure not to fail again
A friend buys a house/gets a promotion	That would never happen for someone like me	Left feeling like there's no point in trying to get ahead with money
Get an unexpected bill	Something always comes up, there's no point in trying with money, I may as well just spend it when I have it	Sabotage budget for the rest of the month

To work on changing these beliefs, we add on D and E: dispute and energising solution.

By adding D (dispute) and E (energising solution), we can take this sequence of events and work on disputing the beliefs that are forming the behaviours, and change our thought patterns to become more optimistic, gradually shifting our relationship with money into a more positive place.

The founder of Positive Psychology, Martin Seligman, identified four factors that go into disputing an ingrained belief:

» Provide evidence that the belief is factually incorrect.
» Suggest alternatives as to why the event occurred.
» Consider implications if the belief is in fact true.
» Consider if the belief is useful or destructive.

Energising solutions are productive reframes and redirects to help you confront the unproductive or unhealthy beliefs and then pave a plan forward. Positive Psychology leverages the benefits of optimism to gently reprogram your brain into a more positive space, which in itself makes it easier for you to confront these beliefs and build a more positive relationship with money.

Let's apply D and E to our existing examples.

Activating event	Belief	Consequence	Dispute	Energising solution
Had a bad day at work	Ordering stuff online will make me feel better	Spend money online and feel shameful and guilty	Ordering stuff online may make me feel better but only in the short term. The feeling won't last and making these purchases could actually compromise my financial confidence	Why am I getting stressed at work, and is there a better, healthier way of dealing with this than spending money?
Pulled money out of my savings	I'll never get on top of my money, I'm going to be stuck forever.	Feel ashamed, helpless, unworthy, don't trust myself with money, vow to do better next time and feel immense pressure not to fail again	Saving can be difficult, but maybe I just haven't found the right method yet	Step back and explore why I needed to pull money out of my savings and how I can avoid that having to happen in future. Did I feel too restricted? Did I forget about an expense? How could I plan for this better in future?
A friend buys a house/gets a promotion	That would never happen for someone like me	Left feeling like there's no point in trying to get ahead with money	My friend was able to get that thing because they had access to different resources to me (acknowledges that part of the belief may be true) but it's only hurting myself to compare my experience to other people's	Can I explore why I feel held back from those things? Is this something I want for myself? How can I start taking small steps to improve my own situation so I feel less compelled to compare myself to other people?

Activating event	Belief	Consequence	Dispute	Energising solution
Get an unexpected bill	Something always comes up, there's no point in trying with money, I may as well just spend it when I have it	Sabotage budget for the rest of the month	Yes, sometimes unexpected expenses come up, but not all money spent is equal. Blowing my budget after one mistake is just my brain trying to relieve anxiety in the moment	Plan to set aside money each month to put towards unexpected bills so I don't feel like I'm sabotaging my progress. Keep this money separate from my spending money so I don't feel deprived

Being able to see how beliefs inform behaviours in the real context of our money can help us start to go deeper and marry these things up from some of our findings from the other exercises in this section.

Engaging with money in a more positive way

One of the hardest things about getting Good With Money is believing that money can be different. You've likely been engaging with money in the same way for many years, and it can feel like you've tried everything. Believe me, I relate to that.

Without the emotional component, money would be simple. Right? Unfortunately, it's this overly rational, simplistic thinking that makes you think you know how to change your reality. But actually, you need to approach changing your finances from within. When you tackle behaviour change from an emotional standpoint, you're connecting with the subconscious brain where decisions are made, tapping into those stories and changing the system settings that inform your financial behaviours. Let's explore some initial ways to put your new beliefs into action and start engaging with money in a more positive way.

Your relationship with money

In modern society, engaging with money is unavoidable. But while being in a partnership with your money isn't a choice, nurturing that partnership *is*. In order to feel good about money, you need to start looking at how you treat money and how money treats you.

In Part 2 I explained how my relationship with money has changed and improved, and how the way I treat it, speak about it, think about it and behave with it has shifted. Where I previously ignored my money, I now give it attention, spend time with it and make intentional plans for what I'm going to do with it.

Where I previously let money leak out of my life and then blamed it for never being there when I needed it, I now make sure I'm keeping track of where my money is going, and that when I need it I've done what I can to ensure it's there for me.

Where I previously made promises to money that I never followed through on, I now stick to the plans I make: money knows what to expect of me.

Where previously money would come to me and I'd just let it run wild like a child in a playground, I now treat the money I earn with respect, and give it the best chance of doing what I want it to do for me by allocating it to the things I want and need in my life.

Building a more positive relationship with money is all about giving attention to the way you interact with it. How you spend it, how you keep it, the amount of follow-through you have on your plans for it, the way you see its role in your life, the way you talk about it, the way you view it, and what you do with it when it comes to you.

Your relationship with yourself

Your relationship with yourself intersects with your relationship with money in all kinds of ways, and working on how you feel about yourself, accepting yourself and eventually loving yourself *will* have a positive impact on your finances. I know, that's a big call, but I genuinely believe it.

When I look back on the times before I was Good With Money, a lot of my financial problems could be traced back to my fractured relationship with myself. So much of my money was spent on fixing myself, improving myself and constantly trying to be someone I wasn't. And that created a cycle of disappointment—with myself and with money—because none of my attempts at fixing myself ever worked. And with every 'failure', I'd feel worse about myself and worse about money, because yet again, money had left me and I felt like I got nothing for it.

Going a layer deeper, the fact I saw money that way, as little more than a means to buy things to make me feel good enough, kept me struggling financially. It meant I didn't have choices in my life, and felt shameful and unintelligent compared to other people. So, naturally, I didn't see my own value when advocating for salaries or jobs. It kept me financially small. And, subconsciously, it kept me in that comfort zone of struggle, which, despite feeling wildly *uncomfortable* with the fact that I couldn't afford things I wanted or needed, also matched my view of myself perfectly. If I couldn't see myself as good enough in other areas of my life, how was I going to feel good enough to be confident with money?

Of course, working on your relationship with yourself takes time, but I do think it's something that my generation and those younger than me are really advocating for. For me, some of it has come with age, but some of it also came from the choice to accept myself. Notice I say 'accept' myself, not 'love' myself. Because forcing the love can feel really futile. For me, acceptance had to come first.

Start working on accepting yourself, forgiving yourself and giving yourself grace—and then see how that can trickle down into your finances. This can come from practising gratitude for the parts of yourself and your life that you love, as well as working on being kind to yourself and treating yourself with as much compassion and respect as you would a friend. Looking after yourself, understanding your own needs and practising self-compassion can have a remarkable flow-on effect to your financial behaviour, and can really work on reversing the conditioning that says you're not good enough.

Opening your financial window

As we learned earlier, our financial window is our view on the role of money in our lives, and our understanding of what's possible. By considering the alternative realities that we can experience when we engage in positive financial behaviours, we can open our financial window.

But what are some of these alternative realities? Changing our financial reality simply because we feel like we should is a futile exercise. We need a reason and a meaning that we can emotionally connect to. For some of us, that doesn't yet exist, so we need to seek it out.

Opening your financial window is all about exploring what is possible when you master your money. What opportunities can become available to you? What happens when you have money saved? How could you experience life differently? How is having money serving your future self?

Expose yourself to what's possible

Many of us struggle to see the benefits of saving money or of being strategic with our money because our financial window is too narrow. This makes reckless financial behaviours much more attractive because if we don't see a broader benefit to holding on to our money, we simply won't bother.

One of the biggest catalysts for opening my financial window was to expose myself to stories and experiences of people who were living a different financial reality to me. Listening to people sharing their experiences on social media, reading books on how people changed their finances (ding ding ding, you're already doing great on that front!) and talking about money more openly with people around us can help us connect to the purpose of money on a deeper level. When we can see what's on the other side of good financial habits, we're far more likely to engage in the behaviours that help us get there. That can be things like being able to leave a toxic job knowing you've got savings to fall back on, travelling more, buying your first home, making a career change, starting a business and working for yourself, or simply having more choices in your life.

It's important when doing this to ensure that you're looking to the experiences of people who are working with similar variables to you. They don't have to be exactly the same, but benchmarking what's possible against people who are working with significant advantages can make the things we want feel more out of reach to us than ever before.

> **TASK**
>
> ## Get to know yourself
>
> I've said it before—getting to know yourself is an act of financial empowerment. And getting to know yourself from a financial perspective is a big part of that empowerment. Here are some questions I want you to ask yourself about money and life. Your answers can be used to further crank open your financial window and broaden your financial perspective, looking to ways money can support you in living the life you want.
>
> *What does money mean to you?*
> Common responses to this question are freedom and/or security. Maybe that's what immediately came to mind for you too. With this question, I really want you to challenge that. What does your answer look like in practice? How would you know that you'd achieved 'freedom' or 'security', or whatever other words came to mind when you answered this question?
>
> *What do you want out of life?*
> I know, I know. It's a confronting one, but asking it and allowing ourselves to actually think about the answer is one of those little hacks that immediately puts us in control of our money, because it forces us to consider the possibility that we can go out and get whatever we want.
>
>   Then ask, how could money help you achieve what you want out of life?
>
> *What's something you want but feel like you'll never have?*
> Calling ourselves out on the things we think we'll never have—and asking why we think that is—is incredibly powerful. It uncovers

the limits we've been living with, without even realising it. While some limits are quite real (hello, housing affordability), others can be self-imposed, and can cause us to keep ourselves in a box and closed off from opportunities. Uncovering what these are can help us connect with the value of money more deeply, and feel like participating in money management is worthwhile.

What does financial success look like to you, and to what extent do you think you'll achieve it?
This question can be a great way to open our financial windows. We often have a wide view of what success can be, but a narrow view of what's possible for us personally. Alternatively, we can have a narrow view of both, not knowing what's truly possible and therefore not believing it's possible for us. Whatever your responses are, see if you can challenge both sides of the question and work on closing the gap between what's possible and what's possible *for you*.

What feels like a lot of money to you?
This is a great identifier of where your invisible financial limits are sitting. It's really common to have numbers in your head that you consider big, often from a childhood experience like a memory of what someone wealthier than your parents earned, or something that your family couldn't afford. I always thought a salary of £25,000 (AUD $47,000) was a lot of money because I'd heard my parents talk about it like it was a lot of money. For a long time, my financial window wasn't open enough to realise that people can earn a lot more than that! Plus, taking inflation into account, my belief about what was a lot of money ended up being a little above minimum wage by the time I was working full time!

What you'll probably notice with your responses to these questions in the task you've just done is minimal references to material things. Any material things that did come up were likely directly linked to benefiting your life in some way rather than just having them for the sake of having them. Shifting your view of money to see it as a resource rather than just tokens to keep gambling on the game of life is an important step in building a positive relationship with money.

In fact, the better your relationship with money gets, the less you'll find yourself associating money with material things. I'm absolutely not saying you can't have nice things when you're Good With Money—far, *far* from it. In fact, we want you to have the nicest of things when you're Good With Money! And you're gonna be able to have them without compromising your financial position, without regret, without feeling like you've messed everything up just to have something you're not even really sure you wanted. But, the more you start seeing money as a resource to live your best life with, the less you require material goods to experience life the way you want to.

That said, we know that the consumption-obsessed world we live in makes this a little more difficult, and so we need to get really good at noticing when we're reaching for consumption as a way to outsource the feelings we want to experience.

Recently I was in Sydney for work—meeting my publisher for this book, actually. It was the day we'd agreed on the title, *Good With Money*, and I'd had a really rough couple of weeks in the lead-up to that because I was feeling completely and utterly lost with what I was even doing with the book. But the meeting had gone well and there I was, feeling like maybe I wasn't such a total failure after all, looking at the Opera House and the Harbour

Bridge (I know they're touristy, but I'm a small-town English girl at heart and I never ever thought someone like me would be standing in front of them while on a work trip), when I had the sudden urge to buy something to commemorate that good feeling. Sorry . . . what? Excuse me, brain. What the heck is going on here?

Now, had there been something I really wanted to buy that really meant something to me, buying it in that special moment of reflection wouldn't necessarily have been a bad thing. But buying something only for the sake of spending some money to try to hold on to that feeling was a plain and simple glitch in my financial script. I'd remembered previous times when I'd used a good feeling as an excuse to buy something, and almost gone to do the same again.

Luckily I intercepted the glitch (and wrote a newsletter about it, obviously) and managed to keep my money firmly in my bank account *takes bow*. But it serves as a reminder that with so many temptations to spend money all the time, even once you are Good With Money, your brain can still betray you when you least expect it. But that's okay. Learning to recognise those glitches is part of what makes you Good With Money.

Reclaiming your financial decisions

One of the most important things we can do for our finances—and our lives in general—is to take back control of our spending decisions. This means fighting back against all the ways we're conditioned to spend, and understanding where our decisions have been hijacked.

From a purely financial perspective, reclaiming your financial decisions can mean you spend less money overall. Yay. But it's not just about spending less, it's also about spending better, and learning how to use money in a way that works for you, not for who you've been told you need to be.

Looking beyond finances altogether, opening our consciousness to the way we make decisions and engage in habits is a transferable skill that we can copy and paste to other areas of our lives. Double win!

Reclaiming our spending decisions starts with awareness of what's happening when we spend money. I've split the process into three zones:

- the activation zone
- the decision zone
- the reflection zone.

When we're Good With Money and we're aware of our spending decisions, we can unlock a fourth bonus zone: the empowerment zone. But before we get to that, let's look at those first three.

The activation zone. This is the day-to-day routine of your life. This is where you get activated to buy things, where your weaknesses translate into temptations, where a bad day can be the catalyst for an online shopping spree, where a night out can send you into a 'nothing to wear' tailspin. This is the place where your inner villains are hiding out, looking for an opportunity to strike you down.

The decision zone. This zone is much shorter, time-wise, but a lot more intense. This is the moment when you decide to spend money. There's a lot you can do in this zone to spend better. When you're Good With Money, it actually becomes the opportunity zone, because it's where you can apply the awareness, intentionality and other strategies that you've developed to make decisions that lead to positive outcomes.

You can add delaying strategies between entering and leaving the decision zone in order to give yourself more time to make the decision. You might leave the item in your cart, or walk away from the shop with the intention of deciding tomorrow or another defined point in time. These delays can help you make more rational decisions if you're finding it hard to choose the 'no'.

The reflection zone. This starts after you've decided whether or not to spend the money. This is where you may start feeling regret, start mentally number crunching what you could've done with that money instead, start weighing up pros and cons, and just generally start seeing things more clearly as reality sets in and the dopamine wears off. It's also where some decisions can send you back around to the activation zone and tumbling through the spending cycle again.

When you learn to reclaim your financial decisions, the way you move through these phases changes. You're far more in control of your **activation zone**, and things that activate you and awaken your inner villain become much less significant players in your financial behaviour. The **decision zone** plays the same role in the process, but it's more like a pet you've trained meticulously than a container of chaos and franticness. The **reflection zone** is a much more positive, grounded space, where you're able to stand by the decision you made—and rather than feeding back around to the activation zone, you can move forward: you've unlocked the **empowerment zone**.

The empowerment zone effectively closes off the spending process and allows each individual decision to exist as an end-to-end process. It acts as the circuit-breaker of self-fulfilling spending cycles that can fall out of untamed activation and decision zones, and regret and shame-cluttered reflection zones.

When you're Good With Money, the empowerment zone is where you're able to own the decision you've made and feel like your choices are within your control. If you've walked away from something you were tempted to spend money on or you've opted for the more favourable financial decision, the empowerment zone is where you really lean into the contentment you have with that decision. This is where you realise that life goes on without having to keep putting coins in your mental poker machine. It's where your sense of financial confidence begins to compound, and where you start to break up with the idea that happiness and that elusive serotonin come from consumption.

Equally, the empowerment zone can be where you reap the rewards of conscious financial decisions that do result in spending money. If you've decided to buy something—because, remember, reclaiming your decisions isn't about not buying, it's about buying *right*—the empowerment zone is where you're able to feel really good about that purchase. You're not torturing yourself, you're not feeling guilt or shame or regret or spiralling back around to the activation zone. You're feeling freaking amazing because you've used your money to improve your life. You've closed the loop.

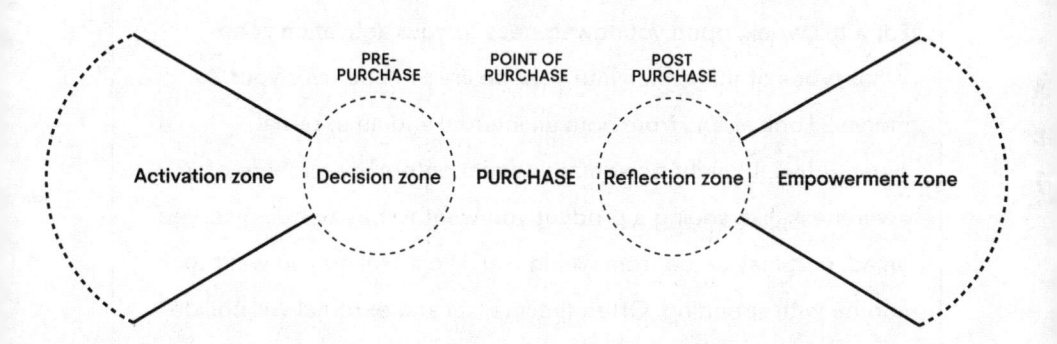

```
                    PRE-        POINT OF      POST
                  PURCHASE      PURCHASE    PURCHASE

   Activation zone | Decision zone | PURCHASE | Reflection zone | Empowerment zone
```

Let's break down these zones even further, and see how recognising your zones can help you to own your financial decisions.

Rewiring the activation zone

Rewiring the activation zone is all about working out what's going on in there. This is where a lot of the concepts we've discussed in this book will come into play, including your identity and how you spend in relation to it, the meaning you project onto things, how your weaknesses are capitalised on and the things your inner villains tell you are true.

A lot of this stuff happens without us really noticing because it's on a subconscious level, almost like autopilot. As we know, our creative director is processing our thoughts, feelings and experiences and making sense of them through the stories it creates. The activation zone is where these stories start to come into play and drive our behaviour.

> **TASK**
>
> ## Auditing your activation zone
>
> For a full week, open your awareness to your activation zone. What types of things activate your desire to hand over your money? Look at this from both an internal and an external perspective. It might be something that enters your sphere of awareness, like seeing a product you want to buy or being served an ad, or it may come from within you, like a feeling you want to soothe with spending. Often the internal and external will collide at some point and drag you into the vortex of insecurity that's being matched to an opportunity to buy.
>
> Take note of your environment and the commonalities in your activators. What are you doing? Who are you with? What precedes that desire presenting itself? Curating an environment that protects you from your activators is a powerful way to change how you respond in those key moments.

> Try looking at your activation zone as a series of dominoes that lead you to the decision zone. What's the first thing that happens? Then how do you respond to that? And then what comes after that? Actions, thoughts and feelings are all important pieces of the puzzle.
>
> For example, it might be that the first domino is a bad day at work. To cope with that bad day at work, you get home and watch TV. While you watch TV, you find yourself scrolling online stores. Then you see something that gives you the feeling of potential relief that you're looking for, and one or more of your inner villains start to awaken as you scramble for the belief that'll determine how you respond in this situation. That's when you start edging into the decision zone.
>
> Identifying what happens in your activation zone is key, because you can't change the processes you don't know exist. Once you're aware of the things that stir up a desire to spend money, you can decide to respond to them differently.

Rewiring the decision zone

The decision zone is where we start to look at those gaps we believe we're filling. It's where a lot of our subconscious financial beliefs pop up to control our financial behaviour—where our villain really takes the wheel. Reclaiming the decision zone is all about bringing those decisions into our consciousness. This can often mean replacing the standard behaviour (purchasing) with something else (behaviour redirection) while also learning how to make *healthy* spending decisions.

The latter is actually the hardest one. While it's not easy to change any habit, giving something up entirely can actually be easier than learning to behave *differently*. As you learn to make better spending decisions, you may find that it gets easier over time to find the 'no', and harder to find the 'yes', because the yes requires you to consider a whole raft of factors, from your financial capacity, to the things you value, to your financial priorities, to what your villains might be telling you. But it's important that you do learn to find the yes, because you don't want to overdo restriction and end up completely unable to enjoy your money.

The three Bs

In your decision zone, you need to look out for the three Bs: bargaining, beliefs and balancing.

Bargaining. We're really good at convincing ourselves of the reasons why we should spend money on something. Remember all those excuses we make? 'This will be the last one,' or 'This will make me feel confident,' or 'I need this thing to be able to achieve my goal.'

What to do: you want to start learning to argue for the other side. Be a lawyer. Why should you get this? Is there any evidence that you're better off without it? Think ahead to how you'll feel after you purchase it.

Beliefs. This is where your financial factory settings are coming into play. You're getting ready to hand over money in exchange for something, so all sorts of money beliefs are going to be stirred up here, especially in relation to that concept of 'keeping' or 'holding' money. At this point, you need to be calling out your inner villains. Why do you want to get rid of this money? Why do you think it's okay to get rid of this money? When you think about saving this money instead, what do you notice?

You might be experiencing a feeling of avoidance—maybe you can't think of any answers so you want to avoid the question. Or it might be a feeling of complacency—'I'll find the money. I always do.' It might be a feeling of 'Why bother?' That's that learned helplessness showing up. The point is that this is your opportunity to start recalibrating your behaviour away from those less favourable beliefs and their accompanying habits.

What to do: listen for any toxic beliefs. Really question your motivation for handing over that money, and replace the parts of your old script that are underwriting those beliefs with your associated 'flipped scripts'. Read from your new script.

Balancing. We've started to look at the decision zone as a bit of a game of give and take, and so to conclude our time in this zone, we need to see where the scales sit. Are they in favour of spending the money or not? That's your final question.

What to do: you need to start getting into the habit of seeing your financial decisions as part of a bigger picture. Contextualise this purchase decision against your values and priorities. What else could this money be spent on? What are the pros and cons of saying 'Yes' to this?

Rewiring the reflection zone

What happens in the reflection zone will change when you've rewired your activation zone and decision zone, but it pays to get really familiar with what a healthy reflection zone can look like. To rewire what happens here, we need to dig deep on some of our past purchase behaviour and identify the difference between a healthy reflection zone experience and an unhealthy one.

> **TASK**
>
> ### Reflection zone recall
>
> I want you to bring to mind two things you've spent money on—one that you regret, and one that you're completely happy with. Take yourself back to the reflection zone period after you'd handed over money for those things, and notice the difference between the two experiences. How did it feel to regret spending money? How might that regret have informed further financial decisions? And then in contrast, when you made a purchase you felt good about, how did it feel to stand by your decision to spend money? How different did it feel to be in that closed-loop state, where you weren't immediately looking for the next thing to buy?
>
> Can you see how some decisions send you back around to the activation zone, and others kick open the door to the empowerment zone? Grounding yourself in the different ways that spending can make you feel is a powerful way to emotionally connect to the outcomes of your financial decisions.

How to move through the zones in a healthy way

Viewing your purchase decisions through the lens of these zones can help you spend better. These zones are important because they represent the practical application of the work you're doing here. It's a bit like driving: you don't learn to drive without actually driving, and you don't learn to change your financial behaviour unless you're actively out there, contending with the experience.

At first, you'll be working mostly in the decision zone, as that's where the ultimate yes or no happens. Over time, you'll become more aware of your activation zone and the path that leads you to consider spending money. As you get better at taming the zones, your activation zone will become healthier, your decision zone will become your well-trained pet, and the reflection and empowerment zones will be the feel-good containers for your healthy financial behaviour.

The aim of this zone model is to help you understand the processes you go through when you're spending money, so that you can recognise them in real time. Learning to know when you're in the activation zone, when you're about to make a purchase decision, and what you're feeling afterwards is key to making healthier choices. When you're in control of where your money goes, you can manage it like a pro.

Relearning how to spend money

Okay, so by now we've got a good understanding of how we make decisions and how to intercept the process when we're spending for the wrong reasons. The next step is to *relearn* how to spend money, so that we can still experience all the wonderful things money can do for us, but on our own terms, and within the context of healthy money management. When we know how to spend more effectively, we automatically make it so much easier to save money. Good *savings* habits start with good *spending* habits—but this part of financial education is often overlooked.

You might be thinking, um, Emma, I am an absolutely elite spender of money, I could compete for my country in spending, I'm so great at it I can almost do it in my sleep!

And, look, I hear you. I also was an Olympic-level spender—I still am. Seriously, gimme your money and I'll spend it for you. That scene in *Friends* where Rachel gets offered the job of assistant buyer and is like, 'I would be shopping! For a living!' speaks to my soul.

But there's a right way to spend money, and a wrong way to spend money. And as we've seen, navigating the modernity of the world we live in with our primal brains and our emotions running the show makes it easy to get stuck spending money the wrong way. When we relearn how to spend money, we can quite literally have our cake and eat it too. We can save our money and spend it too! And I'm going to teach you how.

Let's get one thing straight first of all: relearning to spend money, and getting Good With Money, is NOT about restriction, deprivation or losing out. This is not the bit of the book where I tell you that you shouldn't be eating out or buying yourself a little treat. Frankly, this book wouldn't exist if I weren't motivating myself with the promise of a little treat after each hurdle (and there were many!).

Relearning to spend money is about one thing: intentionality.

That means steering your money ship in the direction you want it to go, and deciding where your money is best spent, where it adds value and, perhaps most importantly, where it doesn't.

ROI-based thinking

Learning how to spend money starts with a shift in perspective. When our financial factory settings are running the show, the way we make decisions is all over the place. We respond to feelings in the moment, we allow toxic money beliefs to dictate our behaviour, we're vulnerable to external messaging and conditioning, and we have a limited, disconnected view of the future that's all too easy to override.

I want to introduce you to the concept of return on investment, or ROI. You may have heard the term before in a business or investment sense. ROI refers to the return you're getting for the money you put into something. Businesses might assess ROI on a piece of equipment. If a machine costs $20,000 but it allows them to make $200,000 in revenue, that's a pretty good return on their investment. Likewise, if you're investing in a company, you want to know that you've got a good chance of making a return back on the money you invested. These types of ROI assessments are generally based on financial return, but we can use the same concept to assess purchases that provide both financial *and* lifestyle returns.

I want you to now consider that concept on an individual level in your everyday life. A big part of ROI thinking in any context is the assessment of a purchase *before* it's made.

We can apply an ROI assessment to almost everything we buy, right from a $20 moisturiser or a $900 Dyson Airwrap, to a $2,000-a-month rental property, a $50,000 car or a $500,000 apartment.

Of course, there are certain things we buy as individuals that do provide somewhat of a financial return. These can be big purchases, like property, or smaller purchases, like appliances, that'll save you time and/or money in the future, so you might do a little number crunching too. Broadly speaking, though, ROI thinking in an everyday sense is much more about assessing the value you're getting from something. This is where it gets really personal—that sense of 'value' can mean pretty much anything you want, as long as it makes sense to you and your overall financial position.

The crux of ROI thinking is really to get you assessing the things you trade your money for to ensure they're worth it for you. It prompts you to explore the thing you're considering investing your money in in the context of your life and, most importantly, consider the consequences of handing over that money. What will this mean for you? Will it mean less money for something else? Is that trade-off worth it? How will this add to, or take away from, your life?

Let's look at a few examples of ROI thinking in practice.

Example 1: *discretionary luxuries like clothing or skincare*

When spending money on discretionary luxuries that, let's face it, are probably our favourite things to spend money on, our ROI assessment is going to be mostly lifestyle-based, but there'll be an element of financial assessment in there too. When we assess the ROI of, say, a $129 blazer or a $59 serum, we need to be asking ourselves the following ROI-based questions:

- How does this add value to my life beyond today? When that buzz of buying something has worn off, what am I going to feel about this item?
- How does this impact my financial position and how do I feel about that?
- What is the lifestyle application of this item?
- What else could I be spending this money on? Am I happy to make that trade-off?

It can be helpful to use the price as a comparison point against other elements of your finances to gauge its potential impact. Future consequences are hard to understand when you're there in that heightened pre-purchase state, so putting processes in place to force you to think ahead can really help with your decision-making.

Some ways to do this are to consider the cost:

» as a percentage of the savings you're pulling it from (e.g. is the $59 serum ten per cent of your savings?)
» against your hourly rate at work (e.g. is the $129 blazer worth five hours of work?)
» as a direct 'this or that' choice between something of equal value (e.g. if the $129 could buy you that blazer or get you halfway to concert tickets you want to buy, which do you choose?).

The key is to see all purchases as an investment in your life. You wouldn't make an investment if the return wasn't there.

Example 2: elements of a trip or holiday

Planning a holiday often involves deciding where to stay, what flights to take, what activities to book, etc. This is a great opportunity to practise ROI thinking.

When choosing your accommodation, flights and activities, you're likely going to be presented with different options at different price points and benefits. A luxury hotel might cost more than somewhere more budget-friendly and simple. A flight with no stops and a better arrival time might cost more than the budget airline that gets in at 11 pm.

Assessing the ROI here can help us make these decisions in a way that works for us. Questions we need to be asking ourselves here might be:

» What are my travel priorities? Am I willing to sacrifice sleep for more cocktail money? Would I rather stay somewhere cheaper to free up more money for activities, or would I rather stay somewhere nicer and have a simpler schedule?

» What collateral costs might each option incur? For example, the earlier flight might be cheaper, but will the time of day mean I need to take an Uber rather than the train?

As with all travel planning, there'll be more number crunching here, which you've probably already done at some point in the past. But seeing this from an ROI assessment perspective helps you focus on the return you're getting for your money, and the consequences of the money you're spending.

Example 3: moving into a rental property

Deciding how much of our income to allocate to rent is a tough one, and often we make this decision on face value. If we earn $1,000 a week, we might pluck a number out of thin air that we feel okay with paying in rent and start looking at areas we've heard are nice. When we instead start seeing this money as an investment in our lives, we can start to assess the return we'll get for that money.

ROI thinking in this case prompts you to think from a bigger-picture perspective. Things to consider in terms of assessing the 'investment' might be:

» What do you value most in a home? For example, location or space?

» What could you get for more money, and what could you sacrifice for less money?

» When adding on nice-to-haves, like a balcony or a spare bedroom (and therefore price), ask: what else could that money be spent on?

» What lifestyle value will you get from this home, and what opportunities could it afford you?

ROI assessments on living decisions have been a big part of my financial management in recent years. We'd always lived in one-bedroom apartments, but post-Covid were craving more space.

Personally, I've always valued space over location. My partner and I haven't ever lived in any of the hot Melbourne suburbs. We choose to live slightly further away because it means we get a three-bedroom unit for the cost of a two-bedroom unit somewhere more central. Equally, if we went even further out we could save more money, but the sweet spot for us meant spending a bit more than we would in some areas, but substantially less than we would in others.

These ROI assessments make your financial decisions personal to you and your lifestyle. Some people get far more value from their home than others. If you spend a lot of time in your own space, or you love a specific suburb, or you really value proximity to your work or friends, you're going to get a greater lifestyle return on a particular property than someone with different priorities.

Thinking with an ROI mindset helps you make better financial decisions, both on a macro level and a micro level. Ultimately, it all comes down to what you value. We'll unpack values more in the next chapter.

Financial prioritisation and big-picture thinking

Our financial priorities are effectively the hierarchy of where our money goes. This applies both on a micro level in terms of our everyday spending and money habits, and on a macro level too, in terms of what money we spend at different points in our lives. Understanding financial prioritisation can help you make all kinds of financial decisions in life, including:

» deciding how much to spend on rent
» prioritising your discretionary spending and managing a budget
» understanding where your money (whether that's $10, $100 or $10,000) is best spent for what's important to you
» knowing when you're spending money for you, and not for other people
» recognising when your financial behaviour is being driven by a specific unhelpful belief
» deciding when NOT to spend money (it's actually the same process, just with a different outcome).

Financial prioritisation comes back to the phrase you've heard a few times throughout this book: you can have anything you want, just not everything you want. When you learn to prioritise, you ensure that your money is first spent on the things that matter most to you.

Maintaining good spending habits

In Part 2 we looked at how our brains often fail us when we're trying to make smart decisions. Experiencing a strong emotion can shut down our prefrontal cortex, leaving the emotional, impulsive part of our brain driving our behaviour—but we don't have to be victims of our primal functioning. We can train our prefrontal cortex to stay online for longer, and tame the emotional surge that causes us to sabotage our financial wellbeing. Here are some ways you can give your prefrontal cortex more of a fighting chance against your emotions and the temptations from the external world. It's all about creating space, distance and boundaries.

Slowing down your decision-making

An important factor in being Good With Money and taking back control of your money is the speed of your decisions. Intentionality is about consideration, managing your impulses and being able to make decisions based on more than a fleeting feeling. It's a sense of self-trust almost, an ability to know what's good for you and follow through on that behaviour.

A powerful skill to master is being able to slow down your decision-making. One of the biggest thieves of our financial confidence is impulsive decisions, and the world around us has been set up to capitalise on our human obsession with instantaneousness. Before the evolution of social media, e-commerce and digital payment platforms, we had to physically leave the house to buy something, or at worst, pick up the phone and dial up a mail-order hotline. (Honestly, given how much I hate talking on the phone, I'd probably never spend any money if I had to make a fucking phone call in order to do it.) We had to wait for stores to be open, and sometimes travel far and wide to be able to go to the store we wanted, meaning we'd go there perhaps once a year. Shops were closed on Sundays, so that was one day of the week we simply couldn't buy things. And forget about delivery.

Basically, there used to be times in our lives when money simply couldn't be spent, and now that's all gone. It's like someone's come along and taken away all the speed bumps on a road, and we're just left to hurtle along without anything helping us slow down.

Learning to slow down your decision-making is your best defence against all of the stimuli you're constantly faced with. Unfortunately, I can't give you a magic pill that will set off a blue flashing light when you're about to make a decision, but like most things in life, practice and consistency compound.

Start by trying to notice decisions you make in your everyday life. Notice when you decide to make a cup of tea, turn a light on, get up and go to the toilet, pick up your phone (that's a tough one). Notice how many things are automatic.

Getting used to experiencing your brain making decisions can help you actively choose to slow down when you're faced with a spending decision. If you can tune in to the fact that you're about to hand over money, really understand what that means and activate the rational part of your brain, you can see your decisions more clearly.

Installing barriers

One way to slow things down is to install barriers around decisions that aren't serving you. It's all about creating distance between you and the opportunity to hand over your money. The most effective barriers you can install will depend on your specific financial habits, but here are some ideas that have worked for me:

» adding things to a wish list instead of buying them straight away
» anchoring purchases to specific goals, or earning out a goal before making a purchase decision

- » having a daily spending limit rather than a weekly or monthly one to make smaller decisions carry more weight
- » simply taking three deep breaths before making a purchase decision and asking yourself if this is in your best interests
- » removing Apple Pay or Google Pay from your phone
- » only taking cash to work rather than cards
- » removing all saved card data from your browser and online stores
- » writing a pro/con list for what you're about to buy
- » arguing your case against buying to increase resistance.

Remember, the aim is to slow the process of you handing over your money, counteracting all the things that have been put in place to speed you up.

Practising delayed gratification

Now, I won't insult your intelligence (or underestimate your previous attempts at taming the beast of instant gratification)— I know you're aware that delayed gratification exists.

But fuck it's boring, isn't it?

I'm not going to sit here and say, 'Look, my darling reader, just soak in this shit about your brain and maybe stop buying stuff you don't even want and start to put that money towards your retirement that's looking to be scheduled for 1 June two thousand and absolutely-fucking-never, 'kay?'

Intellectually, we *know* that instant gratification is our brains playing tricks on us. We know big retail has formulated things this way to take advantage of us for profit. It doesn't make those high-waisted jeans any less appealing though, does it?

And that's the problem.

Rather than lecturing and berating and shaming you for your behaviour by intellectualising concepts like instant gratification, I'm going to help you change your motivations, adjust the way you see the things you want, and make delayed gratification feel less crap.

Sound good?

Let's have a look at what's wrong with delayed gratification. Why isn't it working for us, and why is instant gratification sahhhh much more appealing? As we've already established, it's fucking boring to its core. In the choice between ordering the jeans and not ordering the jeans, it'll be a cold day in hell before not ordering the jeans is a more attractive option, in and of itself. It's the same for cake versus no cake. Gym versus a sleep-in. Scrolling versus cleaning the bathroom sink. (God, I hate cleaning the sink. How does it get so rank when literally all that goes down there is soap and water? Don't even get me started on the shower.)

The other problem with delayed gratification is that we're emotionally disconnected from the reality that comes with it. We're acutely aware of all the benefits of leaning into instant gratification, but the alternative is sort of . . . empty.

What we can do is create a bigger story about delayed gratification. We've talked already about the fact our creative directors are experts when it comes to selling us on the future benefits of something, and while this can have us transferring all kinds of meaning onto less helpful financial behaviours, we can leverage the same function to foster more positive ones.

Breaking the cycle of instant gratification comes down to a three-part process.

1. Fall in love with the alternative ending. You need to emotionally invest in the benefits of delaying gratification in order to ditch instantaneous behaviours and opt for more long-term payoffs. This is where setting goals is really helpful—when you're compelled to give in to impulse decisions, recall a goal you're working towards, or simply the freedom of knowing you can walk away, and let that guide you.

2. Neutralise the pain of saying 'No'. Having something versus not having something—at first, not having feels crap. But when we neutralise that pain, and prove to ourselves that our lives are just fine without whatever material thing we're fixating on, even though it doesn't feel like it at the time, we can call ourselves out on our own bullshit, neutralise the feeling of loss and edge away from the heightened state.

3. Rehearse, rehearse, rehearse. You need to keep repeating this slower, more mindful decision-making in order to reprogram your unconscious impulses. Remember, your habits are what you do repeatedly and automatically. You can make this process your new default, too, if you repeat it enough.

There's a very natural *abundance* versus *lack* mentality when it comes to instant versus delayed gratification. When we seize an instant opportunity for pleasure, we get a dopamine rush, so we associate instant gratification as having, and delayed gratification as not having. The key is to level out that playing field, so that we go from comparing having and not having, to having one thing and having another equally—or, in fact, more—valuable thing.

This transformation starts with connecting to your life, yourself and your money on a deeper level—which is handy, because that's what you're kinda already doing. Replacing your immediate emotional desires with the delayed desire for something bigger, like a big goal of a holiday, or of financial freedom, or of a home or a sense of wealth . . . When you dial that up, you automatically dial down the heat on the thing that wants your attention right this second.

Research around delayed gratification has identified that it's something that can be built up over time. In a 2021 *Science Advances* study on mice (sorry), subjects were able to delay gratification for gradually longer periods the more they attempted it. So while it might feel difficult at first, over time it's something we can get better and better at.

Bloody hell, so you're telling me that learning to delay gratification literally requires delayed gratification? I know, I know. *Hey Siri, play Alanis Morissette*

Behavioural rehearsal

While we're here, I want to talk a little bit more about rehearsal. Behavioural rehearsal is one of the greatest tools in developing any kind of change, especially when it comes to financial habits. Here's why.

In the year 2000, Billie Piper released a song called 'Day and Night' and it was a banger. In fact, I'm pausing writing right now to have a little boogie. I recommend you do the same.

Anyway, the reason I mention this piece of artistic excellence is because a friend and I made up a dance to this song and performed it for her parents. Now, obviously we didn't just decide one day that we were going to perform a dance. We practised over and over and over again, adding in moves and learning which bits were hard and which bits we remembered easily, until we had the final product.

You're probably thinking, well, yeah? Of course you rehearsed it, you couldn't just do a dance you didn't know out of nowhere.

And when it comes to dancing, we know we have to practise. But we don't apply this same logic to our habits. We decide on New Year's Eve that we're going to wake up a different person and suddenly know all the moves to the choreography for a perfect life. We'll get up at 6 am or we'll go to the gym, and we'll just suddenly start putting savings away and we'll never touch them because, duh, we're perfect now.

But just like the choreography of a dance, we need to learn all the different parts individually, and then put them all together and practise some more. When we think of our financial good habits like choreography, we can see the value in rehearsing them individually, and then all together.

Values-based spending

You don't need to stop buying things you want; you need to stop buying things you *don't want*.

Read that again.

This is values-based spending. This is what I advocate for. Part of that requires breaking down some of our spending patterns, ending some habitual relationships we've developed with our money over the years and breaking up with some beliefs we have about what contentment really is.

But the real magic happens when we rebuild our financial perspective and learn to spend in a way that honours who we really are, not who we're trying to be.

A lot of finance commentary skims over this work. There might be mentions of spending in alignment with your values or buying things that support your best self or your growth or your development. But it's harder than it sounds to just start doing that. Firstly, understanding what you value requires some in-depth reflection. But what also complicates values-based spending is the fact that, at first glance, it can look very similar to the exact behaviours you've just worked to dismantle. The difference is that the motivation and intention behind the financial behaviour is completely different.

Before we dive into establishing what values-based spending looks like for you, let's look at some examples of how one purchase can be both a toxic, mindless purchase and a values-based, mindful purchase.

The purchase: a fantastic black jumpsuit for $200.

Scenario one: you're having a crap week and your train home from work has been delayed so you're standing in the freezing cold knowing you're going to be shoulder to shoulder with half of Corporate Australia by the time it shows up. You're scrolling on your phone and you see someone you follow announcing that they've been promoted. Then you open an email from a store you're subscribed to announcing that they've got 25 per cent off for an online shopping event, so you take a browse to pass the time. You see a jumpsuit and think about wearing it to an upcoming event. You start to feel a bit of relief from your crappy day, so you keep browsing because it feels good. You're filling a cart with things (because it's 25 per cent off, why wouldn't you?). By the time you're home, you're pretty much sold on the idea of a juicy parcel arriving for you within a couple of days. You've got a vision in your mind of what you'll look like in the jumpsuit— which is obviously worlds apart from the way you look in all your other clothes because this jumpsuit is a magic pill, right? After you've got home and had dinner, you're back to that cart and the scaries have started to creep in about returning to work tomorrow. To banish that icky feeling, you drag some money kicking and screaming out of your savings and complete your transaction. Boom, expected delivery in two days. HOW EXCITING. You feel a pang of guilt because you said you'd start saving up for x, y or z, but you convince yourself it'll be okay because you've got that $200 coming in next week for a market research gig you did.

Yes, it's detailed, but I want you to see all the micro moments in the lead-up to that purchase.

Scenario two: you're doing a seasonal wardrobe recalibration, relegating your woollens and jackets and making space for your spring and summer pieces (which you've packed away beautifully by the way and are getting jolt after jolt of pure unadulterated joy as you pull them back out of their storage boxes ready for another season). As you go through each item, you're assessing your wardrobe. For a while, you have been wondering whether it's time for a new piece of formalwear to fit a shift in your lifestyle. You've been gently browsing, keeping your eyes open, taking note of styles and fabrics, and you've got a pretty good idea of what you want—and an even stronger idea of what you don't. You set aside some time to either browse online or pound the streets, and you narrow it down to a couple of options, including a jumpsuit. You give it some thought over the next few days, maybe you go and try them on, sleep on it, see what feels right. You decide you like the jumpsuit the best, reach for the savings you've had stashed away for your seasonal wardrobe updates ($100 a month into a saver, in case you were wondering), you make the purchase, and you feel fucking amazing (ahem, empowerment zone) that you've made this considered addition to your wardrobe.

Do you see the difference? On paper, it's two identical transactions. A $200 jumpsuit. If we were being reductive about it and saying, 'Just don't buy new clothes,' or perhaps, 'Don't ever buy clothing for enjoyment,' we'd be missing the point that it can be done in a considered way that doesn't bulldoze all of our other financial goals, and doesn't play into a cycle of consumption that keeps us feeling dissatisfied and hungry for more.

So, how do we get here? We've looked at the actual purchase process as a mechanism for better decisions, but that's really the fixing of the problem. That gets us from negative to zero. We need to add on the positive, proactive part to get us above zero, to help us make those informed decisions.

This is where your financial values come in. Values-based spending has been gaining traction in recent years as women's participation in their personal finances has increased—learning how to spend in alignment with your values is one of the most potent ways of embracing money on your own terms.

We have values in every area of our lives. Family values, cultural values, personal values, character values—and we can have them for our money too.

I want you to think of your financial values as sort of a benchmark against which you measure up different aspects of your financial behaviour. We want to establish the ways that money adds value to your life and honours who you really are. We're all unique. What's 'worth the money' to one person might sound completely preposterous to another. That's why it pays to work out your financial values, because absolutely nobody else can tell you what to spend money on and what not to spend money on.

Understanding your financial values isn't a one-and-done exercise. There are some things you can do to get the ball rolling, but really it's a constant journey of self-discovery. They'll change over time, too, because you're an ever-evolving being. And opening your awareness to how you're changing and how your values are too can help you use money to enrich your life and break up with the consumption cycle you're conditioned to think makes you happy.

Speaking of being happy, I want to stop for a second and ask you something. At any point in this book, have you had a little niggling thought that says, 'I really don't want to give up the stuff I buy?' Or something to that effect? Be honest.

You probably have on some level, even if it was subconscious. Because what you've got so comfortable with is finding joy outside of yourself, acquiring joy through things and experiences rather than using things and experiences to add colour to your existing sense of satisfaction.

That's what getting aligned with your financial values is all about.

Where mindless, reckless or emotional financial behaviour is all about outsourcing feelings to stuff by throwing money at the wall and seeing what sticks, values-aligned financial behaviour is all about considered decisions that don't roll the dice.

Ordering a bunch of stuff online to see if it makes you feel better isn't spending in alignment with your values—no matter how much you tell yourself it is. Knowing that what you're getting is adding to your life and being able to stand by that decision for the long term is what underpins values-based spending.

But the problem you have when making this shift is that it *feels* different. The former feels much more exciting at the time; it's giddy, it's impulsive, it's a rush. But the latter is more muted. It's not a great big splash of dopamine followed by a crash. It's a much more sustained, incremental improvement to your life that feels substantially less buzzy in the moment, but does you the world of good in the long term. Impulsive spending decisions are the fuckboy, while values-based spending is the real-deal partner who shows the hell up for you.

> **TASK**
>
> ## Show and tell
>
> Let's dig into your values by playing a game of show-and-tell.
>
> I want you to start by bringing to mind some items or experiences that you'd consider to be the best things you've ever bought. Imagine it was show-and-tell at school and you had to bring in something that best represented money well spent, or tell a story if it's an experience—what would you bring?
>
> I want you to sit with that question and think about the why. Why has that thing or that experience made it to your show-and-tell?
>
> Imagine someone's asked you to tell them about this item or experience. Think about how it made you feel, why it was so significant, how it added or continues to add value to your life. It helps to write this down like a stream of consciousness so that when you're done, you can pull out specific words that have the most meaning. These words are going to start to form your financial values. The more time you spend thinking about where your money has most potently impacted your life for good, the more you can begin to tease out the commonalities and start to replicate them in your money management system and your financial behaviour.
>
> I'll share some of mine to give you context. Some of them are very surface level—and, yes, we need that because life isn't all about being serious and meaningful all the time. You can get joy from something materialistic as well as something deep.
>
> **My Dyson Airwrap**
> I say basic, you say bitch. Ready? But seriously, I love that little bastard. I bought it in 2020 when I was riding a bit of a financial high from my side hustles thriving and still being in my full-time

job. I was burnt out to an absolute crisp, but financially, I was doing pretty well.

If I were to tell you about what my Dyson Airwrap means to me, it means confidence, it means polish, it means ease, it means comfort, it means simplicity. The product itself is so versatile that it meets me wherever I'm at. If I want to feel glamorous and put-together, it'll do that. If I want to just dry my hair quickly so I can get back to being an entire decade late to the party on *Suits*, it'll do that. If I'm packing for a trip and have no idea what I'll want to do with my hair when I get there, I can just pack it knowing it does everything easily and quickly. The technology means it's less harsh on your hair than traditional heat, so it keeps my hair healthy and maintained. It's super quick and unbelievably easy. When I use it, I feel in control, I feel calm, I trust it, it works for my hair type and, ultimately, even though it sounds shallow, it makes me able to show up as a better version of myself.

My breast scans

There are a handful of people in my life who have been very, very unlucky to be diagnosed with breast cancer in their twenties, and their diagnosis really knocked me for six. I've suffered from health anxiety for many years, and in more recent years it's begun to manifest as an all-consuming fear of doing my breast self-examinations. I have dense breast tissue, and fluctuating weight over the years has meant my boobs feel all kinds of ways, and sometimes I think I can feel lumps when actually it's just breast tissue.

So every two years, I pay around $350 to go to a self-referral breast clinic in Melbourne. (Epworth Freemasons, if you're wondering. It's fantastic.) Everything happens on the same day—the exam, any scans, the results and, in many cases, you can even get a biopsy and/or speak to a breast surgeon on that same day too if needed. They treat me like a human being with anxiety, not a batshit crazy hypochondriac like most other medical professionals do.

These scans represent some of the best money I've ever spent. The process makes me feel calm, in control, safe and at ease. It makes me feel supported. Knowing I can go there allows me to live my life relatively normally despite my sometimes debilitating anxiety, enables me to prioritise my wellbeing and reminds me that health is one of our most important assets.

My Priority Pass membership

I have long maintained a membership to Priority Pass, which is a travel program that allows you to get into airport lounges all over the world. It costs me about $200 a year for the membership, then around $40 per lounge entry. So, yes, some years, if I only travel once, I've effectively paid $240 for one lounge entry. But I don't care one bit.

Having that lounge membership gives me comfort, it makes me feel safe and secure, I get space and time and sometimes a shower on a layover! It means I can work, access good wi-fi, and always get a comfortable seat and plenty to eat (most lounges have unlimited food and drinks). Having the lounge access allowed me to quite literally break my family's generational anxiety about logistics like missed flights, traffic and travel delays. Knowing I have that access means I'm so much calmer and more in control of my travel experience. When I travel long-haul back to England often, and usually on my own, it's so worth it for me.

A stay at a luxury hotel

At the end of 2021, I booked two nights at Jackalope Hotel on the Mornington Peninsula for my now-husband and me for New Year's Eve. If you've never heard of this hotel, it's quite frankly stunning. It has an infinity pool overlooking the vineyard, and everything is matte black and moody. You can drink cocktails lying on a sun lounger by the pool.

This two-night stay cost $3200 for the room alone—and somehow, that was a bargain. I know, right? It was New Year's Eve, though.

That stay was the absolute pinnacle of what I love the most in the world. It had good wine, delicious food, impeccable service (ahem, ease, comfort, simplicity). The space was beautiful, and I really like staying in beautiful hotels. I've always dreamed of it since I was a kid. In fact, I was actually originally meant to go to uni to study hotel and hospitality management because I love hotels so much.

Anyway, the hotel was the perfect experience. It gave us quality time together in beautiful surroundings. It wasn't pretentious and I felt safe and welcome and comfortable. I've realised in recent years that while I really love beautiful places, I don't like the snobbery and exclusivity of them. I used to when I was younger, for some reason. I think it's that trope of the 'champagne lifestyle on a lemonade budget'. I was desperate to get into spaces and places on the cheap but not look like I was doing it on the cheap. It says a lot about my money beliefs back then, actually! Now, what I really value is the ability to enjoy those beautiful spaces without feeling inferior. I like to feel like I belong.

Lastly, I loved that hotel stay for the break it gave us. For the circuit-breaker of everyday life. I love the reset of a hotel stay.

> I love that for 24 hours, or however long I'm there, I'm living a different life. I leave everything at home and step away for a night. I always go home feeling refreshed and like it was worth every cent.

Extracting your values

What you hopefully have after recalling your most cherished purchases are a handful of different examples of your values being completely and totally honoured by your financial behaviour. From here, we can extract the commonalities and begin to understand where you're getting the most bang for your buck.

Contrary to what modern consumerism will tell you, value isn't about getting the most for the least, or getting more and more and more of something. It's about learning to make decisions that pay lifestyle dividends over the long term.

Looking at my examples, what are the commonalities? *Ease. Simplicity. Safety. Comfort. Health. Calm. Beautiful. Peaceful. Circuit-breakers.* See how my values are starting to pour out of that little show-and-tell?

Now look at your own show-and-tells. What are your commonalities?

The more you do this work and the more you start looking at your finances in an active, holistic way, the more you can start to learn how to use money to enrich your life in a way that feels right to you.

That last part is super important. *To you.* To some people, those four best things I've spent money on would be the absolute worst use of their money. Some might say, '$200 for a lounge membership? I'd rather have another flight for that money!'. Their values might be around adventure. Someone else might say, 'I'd never pay $900 for a hair tool. I'm fine using the same straightener I've had for the last decade.' And that's okay.

Updating your values over time

Just like you, the things you value will change over time, and the way you can honour your values will change, too, as your financial capacity changes. I recommend checking in with your values each year, or whenever you go through any major life change.

Beware of the justification trap

One of the major pitfalls of doing work on our financial behaviour is rushing ahead to the good bit. Skipping ahead to the fun part where we get to buy stuuuuufffff. Because we are all consumers at the end of the day. It's going to take decades and major economic and societal changes to dismantle the habitual consumption we've become accustomed to, so we need to be aware of when we're using our values to justify immediate gratification.

Doing this values work feels good. You might feel fired up to start managing your money in alignment with your values. But you'll also probably stumble upon a few instances where you want to buy something and you start jamming it into your values to make it fit. 'I'm going to buy this blazer I just saw because it makes me feel amazing and it's really comfortable and feeling good and comfort are values of mine. Wooooo!'

I've done it, and you will too. Nobody's perfect. Recognising it is the most important thing, because that's when you can circuit break, farm that data—how did you feel after the purchase?—and intercept the same behaviour next time.

Using your financial values to make better purchase decisions

Now we know what our financial values are, we can look at how we can use them to make better financial decisions.

One of the most powerful ways to begin to align your financial behaviour with your financial values is to quantify each of your values into an expression in dollar terms. This helps create a 'this or that' environment in your decision-making, connecting you to the consequences of your actions and enabling you to get more value from your money. Remember the power of the decision zone that we talked about earlier? This is where you can recall your values and make an assessment as to whether something is a values-based purchase or not.

Let's use mine as an example.

- » how could $50 honour my values—that's a visit to a bathhouse (I love bathhouses)
- » how could $100 honour my values—that's a nice meal out
- » how could $250 honour my values—that's half a night in a nice hotel
- » how could $500 honour my values—that's a third of a flight to the UK.

With these numbers, I can now make decisions based on whether I'm happy to give up those things for what I'm getting instead. It's grounding your purchase decisions into your values and helping you to connect to the idea of what spending money really means.

It's all about having a reference point to make the choice clearer for your brain. In Part 4, we'll also look at values-based saving, and explore how your values work in a big-picture setting.

> **TASK**
>
> ## Quantify your values
>
> With the values keywords you've extracted, explore how you can honour these values at different price points. How could $50 honour your values? How could $100 honour your values? How could $1,000 honour your values?

Finding your why

We know by now that when it comes to money, we're emotional AF. Money isn't a mathematical thing—we're human, we have emotions and we transfer those onto money. As we explored in Part 2, those emotions can cause us to behave in wacky ways. But there is some good news: we can leverage our emotional selves to help us uphold good financial habits and develop a positive relationship with money. How good is that?

One of the most important parts of becoming Good With Money is connecting emotionally to money and understanding the impact that it can have on our lives. While our emotions can drive negative behaviour, we can use the same pathways in our brains to build an emotional connection to positive behaviour.

Having a strong emotional connection to what money means to you and why you want to master it can be the difference between success and failure on your Good With Money mission.

Reframing the role of money

First thing's first: let's get really clear on what money is for. We're breaking up with the idea that money is just part of surviving life.

We're letting go of the idea that money is just a means to buy little treats to make us feel better after a crap day. We're letting go of the idea that money controls us.

From this day forward, I want you to see money as a resource. You are in control, you call the shots and you deserve to be in the driver's seat. Now all we need to do is make that resource mean something. We know by now that we create elaborate stories around our money and our worth. Our creative directors have been putting on one hell of a show up until now, so let's leverage that creativity and start using it to build a meaningful connection to what money can do for us.

Visualising your future

During my time studying financial psychology and behavioural finance, there was one piece of research that set my little heart on fire. It felt like a true validation of everything I stood for when it came to financial confidence.

In this study, financial psychology researchers hypothesised that supporting people to save money came down to more than just telling them what to do—by engaging the emotional part of their subjects' brains, they posited, they could help them take on the behaviour required to achieve higher rates of saving.

To test the theory, two sets of participants took two different seminars. The first was a financial education seminar talking about the importance of saving money and putting funds away for the future. The second was a financial psychology seminar in which participants were taken through a visualisation to help them connect to their financial goals. They were supported to emotionally connect to their intention to save money by bringing a sentimental item from home on the day of the seminar. Some brought photographs of their children, others brought trinkets from holidays or things that reminded them of their happiest memories.

While both seminars resulted in increased rates of saving, the financial psychology seminar produced far greater savings outcomes, which was attributed to the fact that participants were deeply engaged with the reasoning behind their pursuit of saving.

Visualising your future is a powerful way to connect to why you're making these changes to your habits and your finances, especially when they feel difficult or futile at the time. Several studies have identified that visualising experiences sets off the same brain activity as when you experience them in real life, which can help you connect on a sensory level to the feelings that the outcome can bring.

Rehearsing using visualisation

Using the idea of visualisation to motivate positive behaviour can take a little bit of getting used to, especially when we've got years of financial conditioning and endless stimuli poking and prodding at us, trying to knock us off the tightrope.

When our decisions are hijacked by advertising and ultra-smooth purchasing experiences, we're battling our inner money beliefs *and* we're constantly faced with opportunities to hand our money over, it's almost a skill in itself to be able to recall what we really want and use it to benchmark our decisions.

A great way to try this technique is to start with finding something you really want to buy. It doesn't matter what it is, but try to make it something you really want. Then, for a short period of time, practise recalling that item each time you're about to make another purchase, to teach your brain the skill of choosing between one thing and another.

Say you've chosen a pair of sneakers. Plant those sneakers in the back of your mind, and each time you go to make a money decision, recall those sneakers and think, 'Do I want this, or do I want that?'

You can copy and paste this same technique into just about any other kind of habit change as well. Find something you want to do more of, and when you go to pick up your phone to scroll, ask yourself, 'Do I want to scroll, or do I want to do this other thing?' Getting off autopilot is all about intentionality, and finding that why.

Your financial lighthouse

I once read a quote that's lived rent-free in my head ever since: 'If you don't know where you are going, all paths will get you there.' Put that on a fucking bumper sticker because wow. So many meanings. I love it.

When we're not connected to where we're going, we can justify just about any decision because all paths lead to nowhere. That desired outcome is your financial lighthouse, keeping you moving forward towards something you know is going to be of value to you.

> **TASK**
>
> ## What matters to you in life?
>
> Money is a resource to help you live your life. There are two operative words there: you and your. YOU are the one that's living YOUR life, and so the way you connect to money is going to be unique to you.

- What do you care about in life?
- What do you love to do?
- How do you love to feel?
- Who are the most important people in your life?
- When are you happiest?

Answer these questions, then revisit each answer by adding in how money can enrich or amplify that part of your life. It doesn't matter whether you're going to end up doing, having or being those things or not for the moment. What you want to work with here is potential, possibility and opportunity. You might want to revisit your answer to the question I asked you at the very beginning of this book, the self-discovery questions you worked through on pages 162–163, or your financial values from pages 191–203.

Building motivation: the gap method

Visualising the future is a powerful way to build an emotional connection to a goal. But we need sustained motivation in order to build the habits that can make the outcome a reality.

There is a technique used in behaviour change known as motivational interviewing, that seeks to help individuals move through the different stages of change and close the gap between their current behaviour and their ideal behaviour. While it's a complex practice, there are some principles we can use in building our own motivation to change our money habits.

The idea is that an individual needs to possess four things in order to be ready to change: desire, ability, reason and need. When an individual is able to express their desire to change, their ability to change, their reason for change and their need to change, their readiness to make the change increases. I want you to spend some time thinking about the gap that exists between where you are now and where you want to be. Think back to why you picked up this book. Think back to the question I asked you right at the very beginning—how would your life be different if you woke up tomorrow able to say you're Good With Money?

> **TASK**
>
> ## Getting to know your gap
>
> Open up your notebook or grab a piece of blank paper. On the left-hand side, write down a few words or sentences that describe where you're at right now with money. On the right-hand side, write down where you want to be. Then, in between those two things, I want you to write four lists.
>
> - one list of sentences about why you want to close this gap (DESIRE)
> - one list of sentences explaining why you are able to close this gap (ABILITY)—don't be afraid to gas yourself up here
> - one list of reasons for closing the gap (REASON).
> - one list of sentences explaining why you need to close this gap (NEED).
>
> This exercise can help build your motivation and increase your readiness to change, by encouraging you to engage in what's known as 'change talk'. In Part 2 we looked at the importance of your self-talk around money. The same principles apply here when talking about your ability to change behavioural patterns.

PART 4

Putting it all into practice

Your Good With Money upgrade is underway. You've confronted your toxic money beliefs, become aware of your financial patterns and programming, learned how to reclaim your spending decisions, explored your financial values, and connected to the why behind your money journey. Phew! You're absolutely crushing this!

What you need now is a system to uphold all of that juicy stuff. Without somewhere for all your new learnings to exist, it can be hard to make good on your new habits and goals. But with the system I'm about to teach you, you'll have the power to actually start making stuff happen for you and your money.

Active and intentional money management

For so long, I was passively running my finances. Almost every move I made with money was an attempt to rectify a mistake, undo what I'd just done, balance out a spending binge or scramble together the money for an expense. I was so rarely, if ever, taking an active role in managing my money—with the exception of setting fantasy budgets that served no purpose other than to make me feel like an absolute failure.

Passive money management is a bit like going to the supermarket without a list. How do you shop without a list? You see the specials, you try to scramble up meal ideas in your head, you might find one central item and then build a meal around it and inevitably forget something. (Ironically enough, I was also regularly shopping without a list before I became Good With Money. Turns out, intentionality benefits several areas of your life.)

It's really easy to run your entire financial life that way, being led by what you come across, spending your money in response to feelings, reacting to needs and wants in the moment they arise without taking the time to think through the consequences of those decisions, and being utterly surprised at how much everything adds together and compounds into a much bigger problem.

Active financial participation is all about intentionally deciding where your money is going before it goes there. It asks you to use your money as a resource and deploy it into various areas of your life where you need it to work for you, from meeting your basic needs to expressing your values to enjoying your lifestyle. It's just like going to the grocery store with a list. You strategically move through the store adding items that have been pre-selected to feed you for that week, knowing what the consequences of your decisions are going to be, and knowing you've planned out how all of your decisions will work together.

It's prioritising the things that matter the most, and sometimes saying 'No' to things to free up money for something else. It looks like looking ahead to what's coming up, knowing what matters to you and how to align your financial behaviour to that. It's seeing your income as a resource to be drawn from—a resource over which you have control.

Active financial participation also means having visibility over what your life looks like, what your routines look like, what your needs are and how you can manage and mitigate risks and unforeseen events. It's essentially an intuitive understanding of your money and an ability to make decisions, recognise glitches in your approach and rectify mistakes going forward.

The foundational principles of managing money

My hope here is to empower you with the understanding of what it means to be Good With Money so that you can adapt your approach into something that suits you. Instead of giving you a cookie-cutter budgeting system or telling you a cut-and-dry percentage of your money that should go to x, y or z, I want to instead help you understand and embrace the foundational principles of managing money, so that it becomes second nature to you.

Plug-and-play systems work well for some people, especially at first. Whether it's a spreadsheet that tells you how much to spend on entertainment or a system like the 50/30/20 budget that says you should allocate 50 per cent of your income to your needs, 30 per cent to your wants and 20 per cent to your savings. I understand that some people find it easier to get clear answers on what to do.

The problem I find with these systems is that they don't empower you to manage money without them. One event that doesn't fit can threaten the whole ecosystem and throw it out of whack.

So, instead, what we're going to do is talk about the principles of managing money so that you can take what makes sense for you and adapt it to your life and circumstances.

What IS money management?

Money management, budgeting, spending plan, money system ... call it what you want, they all mean the same thing. Managing your money is essentially telling your money where to go, and allowing yourself to organise your resources for now and for later. It's as simple as that.

What are you actually doing when you manage money or 'budget'?
Managing money is spreading your money out across different areas of your life. Some of that happens in the here and now, paying your regular expenses and buying your day-to-day things. Some of it happens over the long term, like reserving some money for a rainy day or for future goals.

Do I need a budget?
Yes. This is one of the few money questions I can answer with one word. Yes, you need a budget. But it doesn't need to be drab or boring. We're going to talk about creating a financial ecosystem that you're going to LOVE. *Seriously, you're going to love this thing more than the first sip of a spicy marg, or finding out your fave TV show has dropped a new series.*

Budget myth-busting

I can't spend money
Phooey, this could not be more wrong. You can spend on whatever you like, just as long as it's intentional and mindful. You can set aside money for any of your vices—your budget or your ecosystem just gives it a structure.

It's really restrictive
Wrong again! Managing your money doesn't need to be restrictive at all. You're just telling your money where it needs to go and making life easier for yourself. If anything, a good budget will make you feel less restricted than constantly starting over every Monday!

I have to track every single dollar
Oh, hell no. I wouldn't be writing this book if that were the case. I HATE tracking every dollar. From time to time, it can be really handy to keep your finger on the pulse of your money, but you absolutely don't have to do it all the time. In fact, the better you get with money, the less you'll need to track.

Life is more enjoyable without my budget
I can totally see why you might think that, because it can feel fun and free and rebellious to ditch the rules and live life recklessly. But I promise you, when you get your money management system right (like we're going to right now), life will be endlessly more enjoyable AND you'll get to feel in control of your money too.

I'll be the boring friend who's on a budget
There's a difference between being 'on a budget' and having a budget. Trust me, having a budget doesn't mean you have to be a buzzkill. You could have a budget for $1 million if you had that much—it's not about stretching a tiny amount of money and cutting everything back. It's simply a roadmap for where your money goes when it comes in, which gives you a reference point from which to inform your behaviour.

> Get this in a worksheet! Scan the QR code or enter the URL below to access a printable worksheet that will help you implement the ecosystem in this chapter for yourself!
> www.thebrokegeneration.com/goodwithmoneyresources

Your financial ecosystem: the Good With Money method

Okay, let's do this. Let's build you a money ecosystem that encapsulates your Good With Money habits and makes getting Good With Money and staying Good With Money a complete no-brainer.

Top-down money management

Our Good With Money ecosystem is going to be a top-down approach. Essentially, this means that when our money comes in, it sits in a little imaginary cloud above our heads and we pull it down for different uses. The aim of our financial ecosystem is to have a set routine for how this works. Our money will come into our cloud and we'll pull that money down into different categories like bills, spending, saving, etc.

Before I got Good With Money, I'd get paid and then . . . well, nothing. I'd get paid and off I'd go living my life. My money went into that imaginary cloud, but I didn't ever do anything except let it leak out until there was none left.

It's helpful to start viewing top-down money management like a flowchart. Your money starts at the top, then you pull it down into the next level—spend and keep. Your spend side can then be broken down to encompass essential spending, like your rent or mortgage, bills and groceries, and some discretionary spending too. And your keep side can also be broken down into different savings categories, as well as money you might park for use in the short term.

If you have debts to pay off or BNPL balances to deal with, don't stress. This ecosystem can absolutely still work for you. Go through the steps with me now, and then on pages 241–243 I'll take you through how to factor your debt repayments into the system.

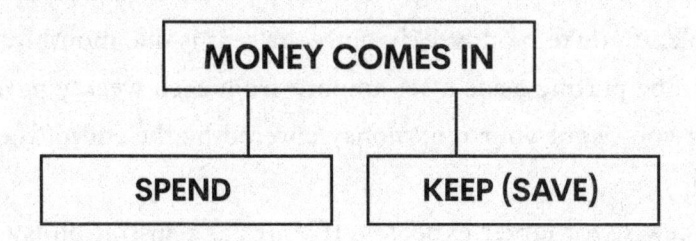

```
         ┌─────────────────┐
         │ MONEY COMES IN  │
         └────────┬────────┘
             ┌────┴────┐
     ┌───────┴──┐   ┌──┴──────────┐
     │  SPEND   │   │ KEEP (SAVE) │
     └──────────┘   └─────────────┘
```

Now, we're going to build out your ecosystem together, step by step.

Step 1: prioritise your essential expenses
Our first priority is to split that total income between 'spend' and 'keep'. To do this, we first need to know what our essential expenses are. This will form the first category under our 'spend' channel.

To do that, we're going to use a technique called expense streamlining.

A good money management system helps us manage our brains better. We know that our brains are impulsive and we love instant gratification, which is why we want to set up our money management system so that it's as easy as possible to do the right thing, and as hard as possible to screw up.

An important part of that is expense streamlining. This completely changed the game for me, and it's one of the most important techniques I encourage people to get across with their money.

What you're doing with streamlining is condensing your expenses down into one standardised expense. That way, it's the same amount every time you get paid, which makes it so much easier to keep on top of because you know that every time your pay comes in, the first thing you do is pay that set amount. For example, if you're paid weekly but your rent is due monthly, you want to be putting aside a set amount from each weekly payday so that you've got your rent money covered by the end of the month.

Likewise for larger expenses. If your car registration is $800 for the year and is due in August, you want to be setting aside a certain amount each time you get paid so that you're not left fumbling for the money when August comes around. This is commonly known as a 'sinking fund' in the personal finance world.

Streamlining is incredibly powerful for improving the way you feel about money. Not only does it help you feel more in control of your money, because you're actively setting aside money to cover those expenses rather than stressing over them when they're looming, but it helps you make better financial decisions too. When you know what your core expenses are in the context of your salary, you can better decide what expenses to take on in terms of cars, rent/mortgage, holidays, etc., and better understand how these decisions fit into the broader scope of your finances.

How to streamline your regular expenses

Firstly, list out all your fixed expenses—these are the ones that are the same every time they're due, like rent or your phone bill. List out every fixed expense you pay and how often you pay it.

For example:

» rent, $300 per week
» phone bill, $40 per month
» Netflix, $15 per month
» gym, $70 per month.

Then list out any variable expenses—things that change based on usage, like fuel, electricity, gas, groceries, etc. For these variable expenses, you need to work with a rough estimate, so you might want to look to the last three months for a rough idea of how much you spend.

For example:

» groceries, approx. $100 per week
» fuel, approx. $50 per week
» electricity, approx. $400 per quarter.

HOT TIP: it's helpful when doing this work to review each of these expenses and make sure you're not harbouring a money leak or overpaying for something you don't use or could get cheaper.

Then it's time to number crunch. You want to work out how much each of those expenses total up to for the entire year. Here's how:

- For a weekly expense, multiply it by 52.
- For a fortnightly expense, multiply it by 26.
- For a monthly expense, multiply it by 12.
- For a four-weekly expense (e.g. it's paid every fourth Friday), multiply it by 13.
- For a quarterly expense, multiply it by 4.

Then, add up all your annual totals for fixed and variable expenses. This is how much your expenses will cost you for the full year. It can help to add a five to ten per cent buffer just to account for any variations in cost.

You then want to break this amount down again to match your pay frequency.

- If you get paid monthly, you'll have 12 paydays per year.
- If you get paid weekly, you'll have 52 paydays per year.
- If you get paid fortnightly, you'll have 26 paydays per year.
- If you get paid four-weekly, e.g. every fourth Friday, you'll have 13 paydays per year.

Take that annual expense total and divide it by the number of paydays you have in a year, as worked out in the guide above. BOOM. You have got yourself a streamlined expense total.

Set aside that exact amount from every single payday, and you'll know that your bills and essential expenses are taken care of as a priority.

HOT TIP: separate this money into its own account so it's set aside and doesn't get mixed up with the rest of your cashflow.

How to set up a sinking fund

We can set up sinking funds for everything from our car registration fee to tickets to the next Taylor Swift tour. Quite literally anything that needs to be paid in a lump sum. Just like our bills, we can chunk these up and set aside an equal amount from each payday into their own account to cover them.

Start with how much the expense costs. If it's an amount you're not sure of, like an annual car service, you'll need to use an estimate, but it's usually better to overestimate than underestimate. If you save too much, that's just spare money for you, baby. We love a buffer.

Let's say it's your car registration and it's $800 a year. Take that total and divide it by the number of paydays until it's next due. If it's due on 21 December and it's currently 11 May, and you're paid weekly, that's 34 paydays before you next need to pay it.

Take the $800 and divide it by 34 = $23.53 per week. By 21 December, you'll have your car registration payment.

After 21 December, you can refresh your sinking fund and take that $800 and divide it by 52 paydays, meaning you only need to set aside $15.38 each week to cover it the following year, and so on.

Sinking funds are not only a great mathematical tool to manage your money, but they drastically improve your relationship with money as well. When you're in control of ensuring you can afford the expenses that are coming up, you're able to make progress with money that's truly yours to use, rather than feeling like you're constantly stealing from yourself to make ends meet. You can manage your sinking funds however you like, either using one account for all the things you're setting aside money for, or an individual account for each thing.

This is how your ecosystem starts to look after Step 1. Your money has come in, and before anything else happens you've set aside the money you need for your essential expenses, and streamlined them to make it easy to rinse and repeat every payday.

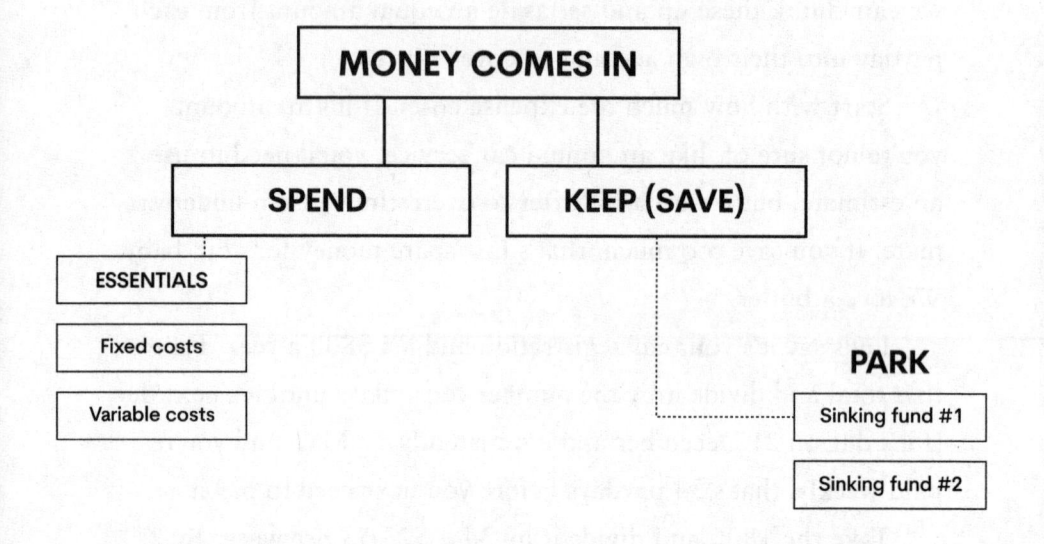

```
                    ┌─────────────────┐
                    │ MONEY COMES IN  │
                    └────────┬────────┘
                    ┌────────┴────────┐
            ┌───────┴──────┐   ┌──────┴──────┐
            │    SPEND     │   │ KEEP (SAVE) │
            └──────────────┘   └──────┬──────┘
    ┌──────────────┐                  │
    │  ESSENTIALS  │                  │            PARK
    └──────────────┘                  │     ┌────────────────┐
    ┌──────────────┐                  └─────│ Sinking fund #1│
    │  Fixed costs │                        └────────────────┘
    └──────────────┘                        ┌────────────────┐
    ┌──────────────┐                        │ Sinking fund #2│
    │ Variable costs│                       └────────────────┘
    └──────────────┘
```

Step 2: establish your workable total
Next, you need to subtract your streamlined expenses, which we worked out in Step 1, from your total income. Let's say $3,000 comes in and you worked out that your fixed costs, variable costs and sinking funds come to $1,500. That leaves you with $1,500 to work with. We'll call this your 'workable total'. Your workable total is what you've got left over after your regular expenses have been accounted for, and this can be split between spending and saving.

HOT TIP: *your workable total is the most powerful number in your financial ecosystem, because it represents the gap between your income and your expenses. If you need to widen your financial capacity for any reason, you will need to look at earning more money, and/or decreasing your expenses, with the sole aim of widening the gap between what comes in and what goes out.*

Step 3: pay yourself first

Our next priority is filling out that 'keep' channel. One of the biggest mistakes we make when managing money is neglecting saving until it's too late. I've lost count of the number of times I've promised to save whatever's left at the end of the month. Spoiler alert: there won't be any left unless we make it a priority before we allocate our discretionary spending. That's why we need to pay ourselves first.

So, we've set aside our essential costs, established our workable total, and we now need to decide how we're going to split that between spending and keeping.

When we look at our money like this, it's easy to get carried away and say we'll save almost everything and live on next to nothing. Overconfidence and overcommitting in this way usually just sets us up for failure, and can lead to the spiral and sabotage behaviours we explored earlier in the book. We want to be playing with different spend/save splits until we find what feels achievable (and then keep an eye on it over time too).

This is where we need to give some thought to our discretionary lifestyle expenses and how much money we want to have available day to day. If we've got $1,000 to play with, what would different amounts allow us to do every week? How do those amounts stack up against what we're currently spending?

It's okay to start small and work upwards. I'd much prefer you to start with saving $100 a month and work your way up by implementing some of the mindful spending techniques we've discussed, than go balls-to-the-wall and try to save the most you possibly can and end up burnt out.

Play with that workable total until you've decided how much you'll allocate to your 'keep' channel. Then, deduct that amount from your workable total. What's left over is the amount you can allocate to your 'spend' channel.

> ### If you have variable income
>
> Having an income that fluctuates each week can complicate your Good With Money ecosystem, but that's not to say you can't make it work. It's harder to prescribe a specific methodology as everyone's numbers are different, but here are two approaches to try if the amount you earn varies.
>
> *Option 1: percentage method*
> The percentage method uses the same four-step process we've been exploring for a fixed income, but rather than setting aside a certain number of dollars, you'll set aside a percentage of the money that comes in. For example, your ecosystem could look like:
>
> Money comes in. 60 per cent goes to your bills, expenses and sinking funds. 15 per cent goes into your savings channel and 25 per cent goes into your spending channel. Then, at the end of each month or quarter, you use any overpayments into your bills category as a bonus payment to yourself, splitting it between your spend and keep channels.

> *Option 2: average and baseline method*
> The average and baseline method can work well if you're on a variable income but you're not experiencing extreme peaks and troughs. With this method you take an average of your last three months' worth of income, and try to establish a conservative standard income to work with that acts as a 'baseline' amount. You use this to prepare the ecosystem in the same way as someone with a fixed income, while setting up an overflow compartment for anything in excess of that baseline. You then deploy that excess through your spend and keep channels periodically.

Step 4: compartmentalise your 'spend' and 'keep' channels

Now we need to give those two amounts a job. Enter: compartmentalisation.

Compartmentalising your money allows you to build quite literally anything you want into your budget—and that's where it starts to get really enjoyable. A money management system can't be boring or restrictive if you have the freedom to literally add in anything you like.

It's all about intentionality. It means you can structure your financial ecosystem to suit your lifestyle and ensure that you're guaranteed to be able to afford whatever matters to you.

But it does require a bit of prioritisation. We've talked about financial priorities and values already, and this is really where these priorities take shape in your finances. You want to be compartmentalising your money in a way that makes sense for your values *and* for your brain.

Here's how your financial ecosystem can look when you build out your 'spend' and 'keep' channels.

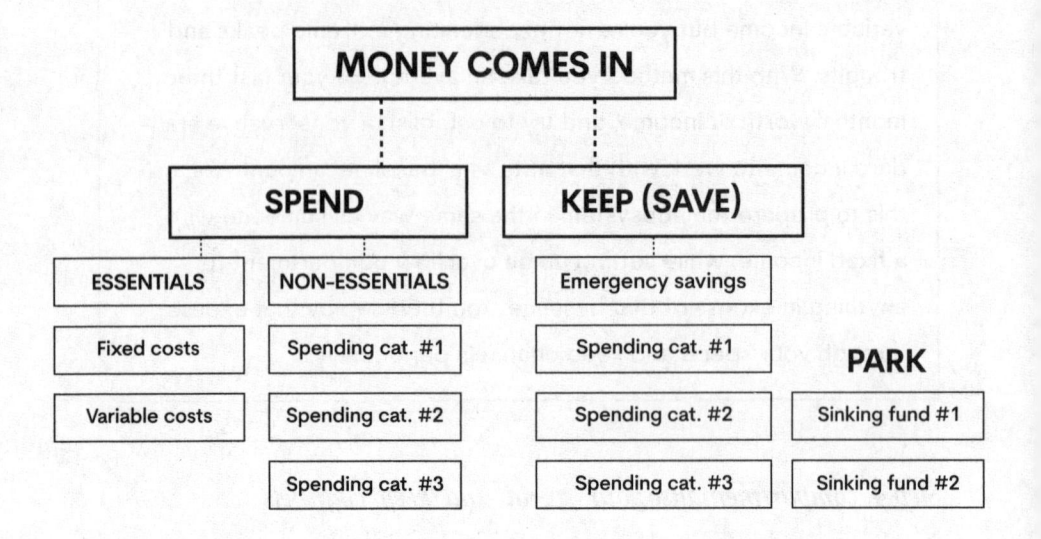

```
                    MONEY COMES IN
                   ┌────────┴────────┐
                 SPEND           KEEP (SAVE)
          ┌────────┴────────┐       │
      ESSENTIALS    NON-ESSENTIALS   │
                                     │
      Fixed costs   Spending cat. #1   Emergency savings        PARK
      Variable costs Spending cat. #2  Spending cat. #1    Sinking fund #1
                    Spending cat. #3   Spending cat. #2    Sinking fund #2
                                       Spending cat. #3
```

	SPEND		KEEP (SAVE)	PARK
ESSENTIALS	NON-ESSENTIALS		Emergency savings	
Fixed costs	Spending cat. #1		Spending cat. #1	Sinking fund #1
Variable costs	Spending cat. #2		Spending cat. #2	Sinking fund #2
	Spending cat. #3		Spending cat. #3	

What we're doing is putting little chunks of money into different compartments for deployment into different areas. We often do this for savings, but less so for spending. Here's how it can look for both sides of that coin.

Spending compartments examples

- **Free spending money**—use it on small discretionary items like coffee or a 3 pm croissant.
- **Personal care/beauty fund**—set aside an amount to cover your beauty appointments or skincare products.
- **Dining out fund**—love to eat out? Allow for it with a dining out allocation.
- **Little treats fund**—set aside a small amount each month to allow yourself a little treat when you need it most.

» **Health and fitness**—ensure you've got money allocated for mindfulness, health, exercise, wellness, etc.
» **Mental health**—we love a therapy fund, gals, we really do.
» **Luxuries**—anything that makes you feel luxe AF.

Your spending compartments should reflect your priorities and values. You can build these into your budget in the same way you build in your bills. If you get a monthly manicure at $70, that's $960 a year. If you're paid weekly, set aside $18.46 each week to cover every appointment.

You can either keep all your spending money in one account and track what you use your money for manually (for example, in a spreadsheet), or you can split up your categories into different accounts. Your bank or financial institution may allow you to categorise your transactions by theme too, which can be helpful.

Payday neutrality

I'm about to drop a truth bomb that might just change the way you manage money forever.

Ready?

You don't have any more money on payday than you do on any other day.

I know it feels like you do, and I suppose in a mathematical sense you technically do. But something I advocate for in personal finance is payday neutrality. You want to be spreading your money across the pay cycle so that the only function of payday is replenishing the money that's flowing around the system. You want to get to a point where your money habits and your attitude to spending are exactly the same on payday as they are on any other day.

The one simple way to achieve this is to have a payday routine. You can do this automatically or manually depending on how you're set up with your bank or financial institution; it's really up to you.

When your money comes into that cloud at the top, it's chunked up into different categories and pulled down into your pots, and off it goes to wait until you need it.

Payday frequency is a hot point of contention when talking to people about their budgets. Many people believe it's harder to manage money when you're paid monthly than it is when you're paid weekly. But if you're practising payday neutrality, it's no different at all.

Say you're paid monthly, and you bring in $4,000 per month after tax. You've worked out that your bills parcel is $2,000 per month, you're sending $600 to savings, and you've got $1,400 left. If you leave that $1,400 all alone ready and waiting to be spent, it's going to be pretty difficult to make it last until the next payday in a month's time, knowing what you learned in Part 2 about your primal brain not being optimised to hoard resources. Instead, you can split it up and drip-feed it to yourself throughout the course of the month. You can set an auto-transfer to 'pay yourself' an equal amount into a spending account every Monday so that you know your spending money for the week.

What this allows you to do is effectively choose how often you get paid. If you're paid monthly but you'd rather manage money weekly, you can! Go wild! If fortnightly works for you, simply pay yourself half of that remaining money upfront and the remaining half two weeks later.

> I personally hold my spending money in a 'salary holding' fund, and have an automatic transfer every Monday at 6 am for my weekly discretionary spending money. It's been one of the biggest game-changers for my money management and my financial confidence. It helps me make better financial decisions because it gives prices some serious lifestyle context, and it means I can organise my money once a month while knowing I've spread it out across the period.

Savings compartments

Compartmentalising our savings is equally important because it helps us build that emotional connection we need to stay motivated. If you've got all your savings bundled together in one saver, it's harder for your subconscious brain to connect on a deep enough level to help drive your behaviour in the right direction. Breaking it down into an emergency fund, a holiday fund, a first-home fund, a Dyson Airwrap fund (yes, baddies) or really anything you like, can help you see your progress over time and make you feel like you're working towards something.

Just like building in your bills, give your savings the same amount of respect. With that spending and savings split we talked about earlier, split your savings portion up into your categories, and send a set amount to each saver on payday. That way it's covered off and you're free to live your best life.

What should I be saving for, and how much should I be saving?

We've talked a little bit about the actual purpose of saving, and how our financial window and our emotional relationship with money can actually block us from understanding the point of savings—especially when the world is on fire and we need to flog a kidney to be able to afford the type of house previous generations managed to own by the age of 25. Sigh.

Saving money is simply moving a surplus of income from one point in your life to another. So when it comes to deciding what to save for, you need to be thinking about what periods in your life you might want to tap into a surplus of money.

Emergencies

One of our least exciting but most powerful savings categories is an emergency fund. That good old-fashioned rainy day fund that you've probably kinda known you should have but never really gotten around to starting. Your emergency fund provides financial support for unexpected life stuff, and psychological relief simply by giving you the confidence of knowing that if shit hits the fan, you're prepared.

Your emergency fund depends on your lifestyle and responsibilities, and grows with you as your life circumstances change. What are the things you need to be able to live your life and do your job? You need to be aligning your emergency savings to these things, and ideally working towards building up a pot of savings that can cover your basic expenses for anything from a couple of months upwards. That way, if you become unwell or run into a personal or family emergency, or lose your job unexpectedly, you've got some buffer there to help get you through. For this reason, it's really helpful to calculate what your minimum cost of existing is, because while you might spend $3,000 in an average month, if you stripped everything right back during a time of crisis, you might be able to stretch your money further.

You also need to consider the types of emergencies that you might need savings for. If you're completely reliant on your car to be able to do your job, factoring in enough to cover either car repairs or even a replacement car (depending on how old your car is!) might be something worth working towards. Equally, if you could live without a car if it died on you, that's less of a concern. How about things like a laptop? Do you rely on your computer or laptop for work or business? If so, spilling water all over yours is probably going to mean you need access to a tasty $1500 at fairly short notice. Equally, if your devices are only used for leisure, that's going to be less of a priority.

Unfortunately, it's difficult to be prepared for every single eventuality, but some level of emergency savings is always going to be better than nothing. Don't feel overwhelmed at the need to save up six months' worth of living expenses right away. Simply starting to set aside a small percentage of your income for emergencies is a great step in the right direction. These little things add up over time.

Having savings for emergencies is something I wish I'd started earlier. Even when I was earning a really low income, I can concede that most weeks I could have found a way to set aside something small like $20. If I'd done that every single week for three years from ages 21 to 24, I'd have saved up over $3,000. At that time, that would have covered two to three months of rent.

Values-based saving

We talked about values-based spending in Part 3, and we can apply this same thinking to our savings. The values you identified on pages 191–203 can help inform some of your savings compartments and align your savings efforts to the goals you know mean something to you.

Big dreams and opportunities

Okay, let's talk about something less scary and A LOT more fun. One of the things I always say I wish I'd known earlier was to save money before I'd known what I wanted it for, and this applies here. Growing up, I never knew what I wanted out of life. Having reached the ripe old age of 32, let me offer you a little life lesson: life has a lot of opportunities for joy and adventure if you're able to put yourself in a position to seize them. Some people are born in that position through nothing other than privilege, and it can feel really crappy if you're not one of those people. But the earlier you start saving even one to five per cent of the money you make, the sooner you can allow yourself to seize some of those opportunities too. The aim is to give yourself choices. Choices you can make if you have savings:

- » choose to take a lower-paying job if you'll enjoy it more
- » choose to take a trip somewhere when a great deal comes up
- » choose to book a last-minute adventure to celebrate something
- » choose to leave a job, relationship or living arrangement
- » choose to start a business on the side
- » choose to move cities or even countries and start again
- » choose to give yourself what you need when you need it (space, time, care, resources).

Let's say you get a new job and end up with two weeks of leave between finishing up your old job and starting your new one. Maybe you've experienced this—I have. But I thought to myself, how great would it be to go away somewhere warm and relax before starting this new job? But I couldn't, because I had no money.

Having some money set aside can help you capitalise on those moments of opportunity that you'd otherwise not be able to entertain the possibility of.

Getting out of a shitty situation

We touched on this just now, but I want to go into a bit more detail on the importance of having money set aside to get out of a situation. It might be a relationship, a job, a place or even just a period in your life. Feeling stuck somewhere because of financial constraints is something I wish on absolutely nobody. Having money set aside can empower you to leave. Having money that's in your own name (not joint with a partner) can actually be what gets you out of a dangerous situation. Some people like to call this their 'fuck off fund', as in it lets you fuck off out of a relationship, quit a job without another immediately lined up, or move cities, towns or even countries if that's what you need to do.

Holidays

Who doesn't love a holiday? Having a savings category for travel and holidays has got to be one of the best things you can do when getting Good With Money. All too often, we book travel before we're financially ready, or we borrow money from ourselves or use credit cards or BNPL platforms to defer the responsibility, but there's no greater feeling than a holiday that's paid for in advance.

Big-ticket purchases

When you need to buy a big-ticket item like a car, having savings ready to go is the absolute best-case scenario. Setting aside an amount from each pay cheque into a savings pot specifically for your big-ticket item can help you build momentum, contextualise all other spending and make better decisions.

Home

Saving for a home deposit is a contentious topic, as house prices continue to soar and the amount required gets more and more out of reach. Speaking from a savings perspective specifically, the best thing you can lean on when it comes to saving up tens or even hundreds of thousands of dollars is time. The earlier you start setting aside a small amount, even before you're entertaining the idea of buying property, the better.

If you're living at home with your parents early in your career, you've got an opportunity to stash more than you would if you were living out of home. Even if you know you're going to want to rent or travel before you buy a property, saving some of your income towards a home deposit before your living expenses go up can give you an incredible head start. $200 a week for five years would give you $50,000—if you don't end up using it for property, that's fine. But you might find it's a nice leg-up for when you start thinking about your future.

Fun money/splurge savings/treats fund

Fun money is exactly what it says on the tin—money for fun! You might have heard of people talking about their 'splurge' savings, a budget category popularised by *The Barefoot Investor* by Scott Pape, and it's a great addition to your financial ecosystem. Your splurge savings or fun money or treat fund (call it what you like) can allow you to make discretionary purchases without having to disrupt your savings or week-to-week allowances. This differs slightly from having fun money built into your spending channel, in that your savings category is more focused on less frequent but larger fun expenses.

You can use these savings for general good times, or be more specific based on what you splurge on. If you love to treat yourself to skincare or clothing or accessories or whatever it might be, you might choose to focus your savings on that category alone, or leave it broad.

Get creative with your compartmentalisation

When it comes to compartmentalising your money, you can be as creative as you like. In fact, the more creative, the better, because your creative savings goals and categories can help build that all-important emotional connection.

Many banks and other financial institutions now allow you to name your accounts whatever you like, so you can really build out a story around how you manage your money. You might have a 'fuck off fund' for your savings that'll help you get out of that job you hate, or 'Ibiza beach babe' for your travel savings, or 'rich aunty' for your savings towards bougie luxuries. You can really do anything you like here!

Step 5: PMAE–permission, margin for error, autonomy and ease

The final step in building your financial ecosystem is to review the flow of your money and make sure you're set up for success.

One of the biggest reasons financial ecosystems fail is because they're unrealistic or they just don't work for who we are as human beings with feelings and emotions. Some of the biggest things I see missing from people's money management systems are permission, margin for error, autonomy and ease. Building these things into our ecosystems helps to account for our human quirks and keep us motivated to work within our ecosystems rather than rebel against them.

Permission is all about allowing yourself to feel like the money management system is working for you. Permission allows you to be an active participant in your system, and gives you something in return so that you don't feel like you're just stuck following a bunch of restrictive rules.

Your values-based compartments help give you permission, as does having some free unassigned spending money, as does setting aside money for something that makes no sense to anyone but you. Personally, the money I set aside to get my lash extensions done every month is exactly that. I know my bills are paid and I know that everything is covered, and I know I've prioritised this over other things and made it work for me. When I book my appointment, I know that my money is set aside for it, no matter what else has gone on in my life or my finances that week.

In the absence of permission, we can tumble into a trap I like to call rebellion spending: spending that stems from blowing our budget, then continuing to blow it on things that go well beyond the original blowout. This can happen really easily when we set our expectations too high, or when we don't have anything in place to mitigate errors or mistakes.

That's where **margin for error** comes in. Your margin for error is your permission to fail (for want of a better word). It catches you in a safety net when you spend more than you planned, or when life gets in the way, or when, despite your best efforts, your ecosystem just isn't enough.

Building a margin for error into your ecosystem can look like having a 'whoops' fund for splurges that take you over budget, or adding a buffer to some of your other allocations that can accumulate over time and support you if you slip up.

Autonomy is something we humans respond to very well, and allowing it into your financial ecosystem can be really powerful. Autonomy is defined as allowing a person to act on their own values and interests, which in essence is what our ecosystems do all by themselves. They allow us to build in things that matter to us, but also give us the flexibility to change things up when we feel we want or need to. The more familiar we get with our financial ecosystems, the more our autonomy will grow.

The last component is *ease*. You want your ecosystem to flow, you want it to be easy, you want it to become second nature. You want to be unable to imagine managing money any other way. The best way to work on instilling ease into your ecosystem is to make it almost impossible to fuck up.

Here are a few ways to do that.

Automatic transfers

Psychologically speaking, we're much more likely to engage in a certain behaviour if it's already the status quo. Studies on retirement savings in places where superannuation isn't compulsory have tested the difference between opting in and opting out of a retirement plan when starting a new job. The research proved that more people saved to their retirement funds when they were auto-enrolled and asked whether they wanted to opt out, than when they were simply offered the chance to opt in.

Applying this same logic to our savings and financial ecosystem, when we make the desired behaviour the standard, we're more likely to do it than to not do it. It's all about making it easy for us to keep doing the right thing—making desired behaviour easy and making undesired behaviour hard. In this instance, it's easier to keep saving than it is to bother turning off the auto-transfer and/or pulling the money back out.

Allowing your money to flow in on payday then automatically flow back out into your chosen categories makes it more likely that you'll stick to your plan than if you left it to be done manually. To double down on this, keeping the savings you don't want to access further out of reach can help. When it's accessible, the temptation is there. But keeping some savings with a separate bank or financial institution where you don't see the balance every day can help you leverage your natural status quo bias.

Round-ups

Some banks or apps now offer a round-up feature, which rounds up every transaction to the nearest whole number (and sometimes adds on a nominated additional amount) and saves or invests the extra amount on your behalf. This is another great example of making your desired behaviours automatic and therefore in line with your status quo bias. By turning your desired behaviours to autopilot, your savings can add up without you even really noticing, which is exactly where the magic happens.

What happens with round-ups is you quickly get used to your transactions being debited slightly higher than usual, and seeing the savings stack up without any effort on your part. I have my round-ups set to the nearest whole dollar plus $3. I now save about $200 extra a month just by tapping my card on things I'm already spending. This comes out of my weekly spending money, so while I'm giving myself a set amount to spend, a portion of it goes into round-ups, which is a bonus to my planned savings.

A new zero

Another way to make your financial ecosystem almost impossible to fuck up is by setting a new zero. Instead of letting your transaction accounts get to zero, you hold a buffer that you treat as your new zero, for example, $100. Knowing that you can't hit zero helps your ecosystem flow much better, and adds in a splash of margin for error too just in case an unexpected direct debit or banana skin expense slips you up.

Process recap

Step 1: streamline your expenses (and add optional sinking funds).
Step 2: establish your workable total.
Step 3: pay yourself first—that's your savings.
Step 4: compartmentalise your 'spend' and 'keep' channels.
Step 5: make it as easy as possible to succeed.

If you have consumer debt

As promised, here's exactly how to factor debt into your financial ecosystem. Firstly, I need you to let go of the idea that your debt is going to hold you back from getting Good With Money. Paying off my credit card debt was one of the greatest lessons I ever got in financial discipline and habit-building, so believe me when I say you are on your way to slaying your debt just by reading this book.

To build debt repayment into your ecosystem, you first need to total up how much you owe.

You then want to chunk up that debt across a few different timelines. The timeline you choose to pay off your debt will vary based on your financial capacity and how much you owe.

Divide the amount you owe by the number of times you get paid in 3 months, 6 months, 12 months, 18 months and 24 months (if you get paid weekly this is roughly 13 weeks, 26 weeks, 52 weeks, 78 weeks and 104 weeks).

Example: if you owe $10,000, you can pay back:

- $769.20 per week for 3 months
- $384.61 per week for 6 months
- $192.30 per week for 12 months
- $128.20 per week for 18 months
- $96.15 per week for 24 months.

*If you're paying interest on these balances, add a 10 per cent buffer to your repayments to account for that.

Then you need to compare these figures to your workable total from Step 2.

Take your workable total and play with different ways to allocate money towards your debt repayment, your savings and your spending. The amount of flexibility you have here will depend on the size of your workable total.

As an example, if you have $10,000 of debt and a workable total of $400 per week, you might choose to put $130 to debt, $170 to spending, and $100 to savings. You manage your money exactly the same as you would without the debt, except you build in that debt repayment with your workable total. With this routine, you'll have paid off your debt in around 18 months.

The reason you set aside savings as well as debt repayments is to help you break the cycle of reaching for debt whenever you need more money than you've got available. It helps you learn to save money while paying off your debt, so that when the balance is paid down, you've got an instant surplus of money that you're used to living without. You can add that to your savings total, or split it between savings and spending, depending on your priorities.

IMPORTANT: if part of your debt repayment includes BNPL debts, it may be beneficial to prioritise paying these down first due to their shorter repayment periods and risk of late fees if you leave them outstanding. However, make sure you have enough to meet the minimum repayments on any credit card or loan balances too so you don't miss a payment due date.

If you don't have enough money to meet your debt repayments, a financial counsellor can help you set up a debt repayment plan and negotiate with creditors on your behalf. Contact the National Debt Helpline on 1800 007 007 to be connected with a service in your state. Mob Strong Debt Help is also available for Aboriginal and Torres Strait Islander people who are dealing with debt.

Sticking to your money management system

Making your ecosystem work for you

We've already explored some of the beliefs and behaviours that were holding you back from being Good With Money. We can now use those learnings to make your ecosystem even more effective, by making your less helpful habits harder to stick to and your healthier habits easier. You can also use your ecosystem to dispute your negative beliefs, uphold more positive ones and ultimately develop a better relationship with money.

The best part about getting deep into your own beliefs and behaviours is that you can customise the way you manage money to directly respond to the things that are most likely to trip you up. Remember: you are the expert on your own life. You know your behaviour and you know your tendencies, and you can use that knowledge to make your money management system work better. As you learned when building your ecosystem, you want to make your desired behaviours as easy to perform as possible, and your unhelpful behaviours as difficult as possible.

Here are a few examples of how you could build out your ecosystem to respond to your beliefs and behaviours and make being Good With Money easy, fun and natural for you.

Factor	Application to ecosystem
Often pulling money out of savings	• Keeping savings separate/harder to access • Giving yourself more free spending money to reduce your reliance on pulling money out of savings
Spending money as soon as you get it	• Spreading your money out throughout the pay cycle and paying yourself a regular allowance
Leaking money every time you leave the house	• Taking Apple Pay/Google Pay off your phone, using a cash allowance
Spending money that's reserved for other things or dipping into funds before you're meant to	• Compartmentalising your money more effectively (using the strategies we discussed on pages 218–243)
Overspending when you feel restricted	• Giving yourself a spending allowance in certain categories • Giving yourself a monthly 'bonus' to look forward to that you can splurge freely on whatever you like

Keeping it interesting

I want to talk about something I call variable intensity money management. Essentially, variable intensity money management is based on the idea that rather than doing the same thing with your money each and every week, you vary your behaviour to dial up and dial down the intensity of effort.

You might be thinking, why the hecking hell would I do that? Look, it's a good question, but hear me out.

Variable intensity budgeting can be really helpful if you struggle to stick to a routine, or if your routine is inherently variable in and of itself, for example, if you're a casual worker or freelancer. Variable intensity budgeting offers you relief from the monotony of standardised budgeting and sees you achieving your financial goals via shorter, more intense bursts of savings, and having more spending freedom the rest of the time.

This can be really great when you're first getting used to modifying your financial behaviour, because you only need to save aggressively during concentrated periods. The rest of the time, you have much more flexibility in your spending routine.

The best way to explain this is to tell you how it works in context.

Let's say you earn $1,000 a week and, using our ecosystem, you send off $500 towards your essential expenses and have the rest funnel into your spending and savings categories. With a variable structure, you might send more to savings one week, knowing that the next week you'll give yourself more to spend.

If you're ultimately going to save $800 per month, you can either do that by saving roughly $200 per week from each pay cheque, or you can do that by saving $50 one week, $400 the next, $150 the following week and $200 in the final week of the month. The outcome is the same, but you're able to dial up and dial down your savings behaviour and take your foot off the gas every so often.

I found this structure particularly helpful when I was starting out with managing my money and learning to save, because it meant I could mix it up and keep myself interested while I practised my good habits. If you find it hard to follow through without existing momentum, you might find this really handy.

You can set aside your 'lean week' each month and keep your social plans to a minimum, cook at home, catch up on some housework and read a book from the stack on your bedside, and the following week have double the spending money without sacrificing on savings progress.

Experiment and hypothesise

One of the best ways to make your ecosystem work for you is to actually experience it. Within your ecosystem, you can set up micro experiments and test hypotheses about the changes you're making.

Let's look at an example.

Hypothesis: if I give myself an extra $50 each week to spend on whatever I like, I'll feel more positive about money and feel less like I want to blow my savings on stuff I don't really need.

Your experiment would then be to give yourself that extra $50 to spend for a couple of weeks, then check in with the results afterwards. How did it feel? What did you use the extra $50 for? Did the cravings for online splurges quiet down, or not?

From there, you can farm that data to decide whether to implement the extra $50 a week for good, or try something else.

Through trial and error, you get to make your money ecosystem work for you in any way that you like.

Reviews and check-ins

Reviews and check-ins are a critical part of your Good With Money routine. Looking back and reflecting on where your money went and, most importantly, how you felt about your finances during a certain period can really help you tweak your ecosystem over time and make it something that works perfectly for your lifestyle.

Reviews involve looking at the behaviour of your money. What is it being spent on, what's happening in your transactions, is there anything that needs attention—this is where you might spot a banana skin. You then want to marry up this behaviour with a reflection on how you felt about money during this period of time, and any external things that could have impacted your financial behaviour or emotions.

Reviews also allow you to keep your finger on the pulse of your money. It's really that visibility component that can help you spot money leaks (like a subscription you don't use or forgot to cancel) or a habitual spend that's really added up over time and presents an opportunity to free up some extra money. You can also check in on your savings balances and make sure that any sinking funds or streamlined expenses are tracking okay.

Banana skins

We've talked about banana skins a little bit already, but let's look at them in more detail. These are little traps that slip you up and put your whole budget into jeopardy if they're not dealt with. Banana skins can be things like:

- » It's your friend's birthday and you forgot to buy a gift or allocate money for the dinner and drinks.
- » Taylor Swift announces her tour mid–pay cycle (if you know, you know).
- » An expense you've budgeted for is higher than expected.

- » You end up having to book an expensive appointment due to illness or injury (shoutout to the thumb tendonitis I developed while writing this book that cost me $400 in hand specialist appointments!).
- » A friend or family member gets some great news (or something shit happens) and you need to race round there and pop either the bubbles or the lid of a tub of Ben and Jerry's.

Mitigating banana skins is all about visibility. When we're connecting our finances and our lives, we're across where our money is going and we're aware and intentional—we have the ability to look ahead and spot those banana skins before they derail us, or learn from them if they do.

Here are some ways of mitigating banana skins:

- » Looking at your month ahead, realising you have a lot of social events because of birthdays, and tweaking your spend/save allocation to ensure you've got the money ready to enjoy without worry. If you don't have the money, this gives you the time to make the changes you need to meet your commitments.
- » Contributing a small amount each week to a miscellaneous fund so that you can cover unexpected appointments or gifts at the last minute.

If you don't have a system set up to mitigate your banana skin moments, that's totally fine. The magic comes from being able to spot something that's slipped you up and ensuring it doesn't slip you up in the future. You might set up these separate savings categories after you've been slipped up by a banana skin in the past.

My husband and I now factor a gifts budget into our weekly expenses allocation, because we realised that birthdays—and the

$50 per person we contribute to gifts—were always creeping up on us. Now, we've mitigated that banana skin and we can withdraw the cost of gifts from our expenses fund.

How to review your financial ecosystem

Step 1: start with how you feel
When talking about money, we often overlook how things feel. Your numbers might be jacked and juicy but if you felt like burning hot trash, that's not something you want to keep around. Tuning into how you felt during the period you're reviewing is really important and can help you make changes to your budget that you'll actually be able to stick to.

Look out for times you felt negative about money, fearful, stressed, overwhelmed, restricted in your spending, disconnected from what you were trying to do, etc. It's also helpful to see if you can recall any patterns of behaviour, for example, being tempted to spend money when scrolling late at night, or wanting to throw the towel in after a hard day.

You might uncover a glitch that's holding you back, or you might be able to weave in some more permission, autonomy, ease or margin for error to help your system run more smoothly.

Step 2: give context to the period of time
Looking outside of the numbers once again, it's helpful to consider the period you're reviewing from a life perspective too. What was going on during that time? Was it hectic at work? How was your mental health? Was it a big season of weddings, birthdays or other events? Giving context to your financial behaviour can help you

connect more to how money needs to fit into your life, and how you can use it as a resource to better serve you.

Step 3: review and rank
Okay, NOW we're going to look at the numbers! Look at where your money went, all your transactions, and then run through a joy ranking (we discussed this on page 134).

A joy ranking involves ranking each of your transactions out of ten against how much joy it added to your life, of course omitting non-negotiables like rent. More high numbers mean your money is adding to your life, but more low numbers mean you could be leaking money or using your money ineffectively.

It's also worth doing a sweep of any regular expenses here to ensure you're not missing any opportunities to cut something out. I always recommend looking for what I call high-impact, low-sacrifice savings (HILSS)—things you can trim or skim out of your financial routine without really having to give much up.

Examples of these include cutting out money leaks (like those top-up supermarket shops!), switching something to an annual payment rotation if it costs less or swapping a product out for a cheaper alternative without compromising on how it makes you feel.

You might want to use the money leak litmus test from page 137 here if you think leaks could be a big part of what's impacting your ecosystem.

Step 4: what went well, what didn't, any patterns
First you want to look at what went well—noticing what parts of your budget worked for you is really important as you can use that to inform tweaks you make later.

Then, what didn't go well? Were any of your estimated numbers off? Did you overspend in a certain area? Did an unexpected expense come up?

Finally, are there any patterns emerging? Noticing patterns of behaviour can help you identify ways to intercept the cycle. Are you always buying lunch on your office days? Did you spend more on payday than on other days? Are you pulling money out of your savings pots?

Step 5: look ahead for banana skins

Next, you want to look ahead to the week/month in front of you and scan for any banana skins. Looking at your calendar or schedule can be handy here. If you spot anything that hasn't been accounted for, whether it's a specific thing like a gift for a friend, or a more general area like a potential need for more spending money for the month, take note of it.

Step 6: make tweaks to your system if necessary

Lastly, deploy these learnings into the ecosystem by making any necessary changes. I know this sounds like a lot, but don't feel you have to nail everything every single time. All we're trying to do here is get you engaged with your money, spot patterns and tweak your system to better accommodate them.

Over time this will become much more intuitive. For example, if you've looked ahead and realised you've got a birthday next week and you need to buy a gift, you're giving yourself the opportunity to plan in advance how much you'll spend and where the money will come from, rather than stressing and scrambling in the moment. Equally, if you've seen you've got a busy week at work coming up at the end of the month, you can consciously decide that you'll prioritise making life easier for yourself, perhaps planning to spend extra on Uber Eats that week. It's all about setting yourself up for success and carving out a little time for yourself and your money—like dating!

Reviewing your finances is essentially like farming data. The visibility that's embedded in being Good With Money means you can see what's going on in your finances and respond to it. It's not about being perfect all the time; it's about knowing how to respond when something slips.

> **TASK**
>
> ## SWOT analysis of your financial behaviour
>
> I love a SWOT—especially when it comes to money. When reviewing larger chunks of time, like quarters, half years or full years, a SWOT can help you identify areas for improvement and ways to use your strengths to capitalise on them.
>
> Draw a matrix on a page with four quadrants. In the top left quadrant write *Strengths*, in the top right write *Weaknesses*, in the bottom left write *Opportunities* and in the bottom right write *Threats*.
>
> Fill in your quadrants with your strengths, weaknesses, opportunities and threats as they relate to money. Your strengths and weaknesses are internal things like behavioural patterns, things you find easy, things you find hard, etc. Opportunities and threats are external things that aren't so much in your control, but things that you can mitigate or capitalise on.
>
> Let's look at an example.

Strengths

- Keeping to weekly spending allowance really well
- Using spending categories feels really good
- Getting better at walking away from things that tempt me to purchase
- Have been building up regular savings without touching them

Weaknesses

- Seeing things to buy on social media is what tempts me the most
- A couple of times this quarter I have gone for drinks after work and spent more than I planned
- I'm struggling a bit with setting aside money for unexpected expenses, because having the money there makes me feel like it's savings that I can use for other things

Opportunities

- Winter is coming up so it's an opportunity to stay inside doing cosy wholesome things rather than being out and about spending like I did in the summer. I could save some extra money here by cutting back a little, like a mini 'hibernation'
- I could start that side hustle I've been thinking about and maybe earn some extra cash
- My wage is going up $3,000 at the end of the financial year so I have $20 extra in each pay that I can use for something else. I can plan this out before I get the money so that I maximise its value

Threats

- Winter clothes are my favourite (jumpers, coats, etc.), so seeing things online will be hard to say 'No' to
- I'm going back into the office more often so there's more temptation to spend money during the work day on lunches and treats, especially when other people are doing it too
- I have my car service coming up and I need to start thinking about how I'll handle the expense if it needs repairs

> Your SWOT analysis can help you set goals for the upcoming year, half year or quarter and find ways to utilise your strengths, overcome your weaknesses, capitalise on opportunities and mitigate your threats.

The system only works if you do

You probably know by now I'm not one for tough love, but this is the one time you'll get it from me. The system won't work if we don't—and this can be where a lot of budgets fall apart, because we think that simply setting things up is all we need to do. While this system makes every effort to help us personalise it to our own needs and install permission, margin for error, autonomy and ease so it can handle our humanness, there needs to be input from us as the users.

If we're giving ourselves money to spend and then going out there and spending more than that repeatedly, without changing anything, the system won't work. It's designed to weather mistakes, slip-ups, life stuff and brain glitches, but it can't do the thing for us.

When we're out in the wild with our money ecosystem, we still need to remember everything we've learned. We need to master our brains, reclaim our decision-making, and solidify that emotional connection to our money goals to make sure we can uphold the habits that keep our ecosystem ticking along.

How to keep your habits in check

RICA

Remember your Good With Money identity and monitor your self-talk. When you're Good With Money, you'll make good decisions. Ask yourself, 'Is this what someone who is Good With Money would do?'

When you're tempted to blow your budget, remember RICA: recall, identify, call out, argue.

The first step is to **recall** a vision of something you want in life, a goal or an expression of your values. Bringing your long-term vision to the forefront of your mind helps you create the 'this or that' scenario. Remember, creating consequences is key. When you bring this vision into the equation, you're able to weigh up the respective value of pleasing your current self, or prioritising your future self.

Then, **identify** the gap you're trying to fill. Ground yourself in point A, the now, and establish what that point B looks like. What are you trying to achieve with this purchase? Is it a toxic expectation? Is it emotional or mindless? Does the benefit last longer than today? Recall your financial values—how does this fit with them?

Next, **call out** your BS. This is your justification filter. Consider this part a little speed bump to help you avoid justifying any behaviour that you don't want to face up to.

Lastly, **argue** the case for future you. Do you really need this? What are the cons of buying this? What would you be taking away from future you?

Then balance the scales. What's your decision? Will you buy? Or will you walk away?

Slow down your decision-making and create distance between you and the behaviours that you know keep you stuck. Remember your behavioural replacements and your redirects—make it harder to sabotage by delaying decision-making until your rational brain is online.

> ### Audit your environment
>
> If you're falling back on old behaviours, keep an eye out for those activators and do what you can to remove them. Unsubscribe, unfollow, hit that mute button, flag that you don't want to see those ads anymore.
>
> When you see ads on social media, you can usually mark them as 'not interested'. Look for the three dots around the piece of content and select 'Don't show me this ad again'. This is really helpful for that pesky remarketing that gets your favourite stuff to follow you around the internet.

The Ultimate Mission

One of the toughest things about making effective financial decisions in the modern world is oversupply. There are so many versions of every single thing we could ever want, and countless stores selling a whole raft of things that are similar but different to the store next door.

How many times have you gone and bought something only to discover the next day, week or month that you're tempted by a similar thing? Let's say you go out to buy a black blazer. Seems like a simple feat, right? How many different types of black blazer are there?

Turns out, a lot. Different lengths, fabrics, cuts, styles, shapes, qualities, necklines, pocket sizes. You can go out, pick up a black blazer you like, only to find that a couple of days later you're tempted by something similar.

This constant revolving door of consumption keeps us stuck in a cycle of never being truly satisfied. The external world will always present options for more and more and more—and this is something fairly new for our brains to have to process.

An antidote to this is what I like to call the Ultimate Mission.

The Ultimate Mission is all about raising the bar for the things we buy. We go into every consumption experience on a mission to find the ultimate version of whatever it is we're buying, refusing to settle for anything less than bang-on what we want.

Why is this important?

Firstly, setting out to buy the perfect thing is a lot harder than buying any old thing that gets you momentarily excited. It requires research, consideration, comparison and, most importantly, time.

It requires you to slow the F down and think through what you're about to trade your money for.

Secondly, when you do buy the ultimate thing, the one and only, you're essentially making a commitment to that thing. You're getting up onto a little step ladder and shouting to the world, 'I am going to buy this black blazer and because it is the ultimate black blazer for me, I will not be buying any other black blazers for the foreseeable future!' By making this commitment to that item, you're forced to think through your purchases far more than you're otherwise encouraged to, because you're actively trying to not want anything else.

Next time you're deciding to purchase something, try the Ultimate Mission.

Prove before you purchase

One of my most popular tips I've ever shared on social media was this one: prove before you purchase. I actually learned the foundations of this from my mum, but it wasn't until adulthood that I applied it to my finances.

When I was about thirteen, there was this brand that eeeeveryone wanted called Bench. The full stop was part of the brand name. Bench. Dot. It was a surf-skate brand, which was of course the absolute moment of the early noughties. All their stuff had thumbholes in the arms and big branded logos across the back. Vulgar, on reflection, but the teenage heart wants what it wants. Anyway, somehow I'd come to see a Bench. coat I wanted, and even my mum had fallen in love with it and said I could have it. I couldn't believe my luck.

Once we got it home, I was already deep into the fantasy of how freaking cool I was going to look in it when I got to school, but my bubble soon burst when my mum announced that she was going to make me wear my ugly-ass cream puffer coat for a full week before I could wear the Bench. one. Her argument? I didn't wear my current coat, so why would I wear my new one?

Ughhhhhhhhh. I was pissed and so irritated that she couldn't comprehend the reason I didn't wear my existing coat was because it was FUGLY and made me look like an old lady. OBVIOUSLY I would wear the Bench. coat because it was hot as fuck. (To be clear, it was not. But I felt like it was at the time.)

Anyway, I wore the ugly coat for a week, and the next week she gave me back my Bench. coat. But once I got older and got my head out of my arse, what stuck with me was the value that lay in proving to myself I'd actually follow through on something before spending my money on it.

I implore you to implement this in your own life. Before you spend money on anything, prove to yourself that you'll actually engage in the behaviours required to use that item. Don't get caught up in the identity at stake. Notice when it's a reactive purchase decision brewing and work to shift it into more of a proactive space—prove to yourself that you've got the follow-through.

Before you buy those yoga pants, do yoga in your pyjamas on a towel in your living room for a week.

Journal on one of the many notebooks you've probably already got lying around for a week before you buy a new one. If it's the prompts you want, copy them onto scrap paper and use them before you hand over your money.

Go to the beach in your less cute bathers before you jump to buy a new pair for the season because you think it'll make you go to the beach.

Proving before you purchase calls you on your ego and ups the stakes so that you're only handing over your money for something you'll actually commit to.

The Tomorrow Rule

The Tomorrow Rule is a little hack that will help you trick your brain into thinking you're giving it exactly what it wants. Creating barriers between you and spending opportunities, as we've discussed earlier, is one great way to get back in the driver's seat of where your money goes, but sometimes, that hunger to hand over your dollars really just won't quit. This is where the Tomorrow Rule is really helpful.

What we do is, when we're on the brink of making a purchase we simply say, 'I'll get this tomorrow.' Make yourself believe it too. Think about how and when you'll buy it tomorrow, think about how great it's going to feel. And then *walk away*.

The reason this is so powerful is because of language and framing. A common rule that people live by is waiting 24 or 48 hours before buying something—and, in essence, this is the same thing. The difference is the way we're framing the rule. Instead of telling ourselves, 'No, we can't buy that, we have to wait for x amount of time,' we're giving ourselves permission. We're saying, 'Hey, you're right, this is a great thing, let's come back and get it tomorrow.' It's a subtle difference, but it's much gentler than telling ourselves to wait. We know shoulding and shaming and 'no' don't get us anywhere. They can fuel rebellion spending, or simply not work. When we accept ourselves as we are and say 'Yes' to ourselves, using a 'but not until tomorrow' to add intention to the decision, we reduce the tension and psychological discomfort that we feel.

The idea here is that by giving ourselves permission to spend the money tomorrow, we're delaying the decision, adding distance between us and that heightened state and, with any luck, by tomorrow we'll have simmered down and our prefrontal cortex will be back online.

Now, yes, there's a risk that we actually do go back tomorrow and make that purchase—there are no guarantees with any attempt at behaviour change. And if you do buy it? That's totally okay. All is not lost. We're not aiming for perfection here. If this rule doesn't land with you, that's okay: you can use that information going forward.

But give it a try first and see how your brain reacts.

Intuitive money management

Intuitive money management is about having an intrinsic connection to, and understanding of, your financial situation, your values, your priorities and what fits into them.

When I first started getting Good With Money, I was a lot more hands-on with my financial ecosystem. I tracked where my money went, I had my eyes on the numbers much more often, I'd consider my spending decisions far more closely. But over time, as you get more familiar with your ecosystem and your spending habits and your purpose for managing money, you don't need to pay such close attention. You'll find you intuitively know how often you can eat out while remaining within budget. You'll find you intuitively know how often you can afford a little splurge on a new outfit. You'll find you intuitively know which types of behaviour work in your system and which don't.

Essentially, you'll develop an understanding of your own financial capacity, and you'll be able to live life much more freely because you've built up that experience and sense of self-trust.

Repetition and momentum are the two key things that will move you closer to being able to manage your money intuitively.

Remember, our habits are the things we do over and over again. When we use our ecosystem over and over again it becomes a habit, and the behaviours we at first have to put effort into sticking with eventually become our new standard way of operating. And, over time, we'll develop a sense of awareness around our money that allows us to be more hands-off if we want to. In sailing, an experienced sailor knows the direction of the wind at all times, and they have strategies that they use to predict the direction the wind will blow 30 seconds from now. That's the type of intuitive understanding we want to develop around our money.

When you're first sticking to a spending allocation and you're getting used to developing that payday routine, it's going to feel a lot more hands-on, and your progress markers are going to be at a much more introductory level. For example, your new savings account might have a balance of a couple of hundred bucks at first, but over time, as you build momentum, that balance goes up and up and up and you begin to get used to living below your means and watching that number climb.

Just like negative cycles of behaviour can compound, positive behaviour compounds too. When you start seeing results, you're motivated to keep going. Plus, the bigger your results, the more of a general margin for error you have. If you slip up in the third week of your ecosystem, the percentage impact that has on your progress is substantially larger than if you slip up after a year of sticking with your Good With Money habits.

As you become more familiar with your financial ecosystem and you start to see it working and all the different compartments getting replenished, and you get to that first bill payment and the money's there, you'll start to experience a sense of peace that you've not previously had with your money. When an expense comes up and you've got the money already set aside. When you see something you want and you've got the splurge savings right there. When you decide to throw caution to the wind and go and have an Aperol spritz with your co-workers in the summer knowing you've got the money in your account and it won't derail your weekend plans.

There's a point at which it just clicks. I promise you it will happen eventually. It's like learning to drive—at first, you're putting in so much effort to remember to do all the things right, but eventually you're able to relax while serenading the freeway with a word-perfect rendition of 'Super Bass' without a second thought.

My point is, this type of ecosystem does take some getting used to, but when you get it right, it's the beginning of the rest of your life.

Speaking of the rest of your life . . .

PART 5

Get ready for the rest of your life

Oh my goodness, we made it! You've got the tools, techniques and awareness you need to get really freaking Good With Money, and I believe in you. Now it's time to look ahead to the rest of your life.

Of course, getting Good With Money takes time, and you'll get better and better with money the more you keep committing to the things you've learned in this book. When you focus on those two simple things we've talked about over and over again—awareness and intentionality—your behaviour will gradually change from the inside, and the Good With Money habits and systems will become second nature to you.

Eventually you'll see your financial situation changing as a result: your savings balance will go up, your ability to hold on to money will get stronger and stronger, and you'll have paid off debts and stopped finding yourself constantly stuck in that cycle of sabotaging and starting over again.

But what happens next?

Being Good With Money means developing the foundational understanding of how to manage money, upheld by healthy beliefs and behaviours that allow you to interact with money differently. But once you've mastered it, there are so many more things that you can do with money. This is the beginning of your journey, not the end.

In this final section, we're going to talk about the rest of your life. Where you go once you've nailed your habits and behaviours, and how you can use what you've learned to create a happy, fulfilled, purposeful and financially free life that serves you long into the future.

Becoming the main character of your money

Just by reading this book, you're already better with money than you were before. Take a second to soak that in. You should be so proud for making this commitment to yourself.

Getting Good With Money changes you. It changes your identity a little bit. And the better you get with money, the more it changes you for the better. I want to prepare you for that change, because it really is quite wonderful.

Feeling like you're not Good With Money really fucking sucks. I was there for such a long time, and I know that so many of us are harbouring a shameful financial past, or a sense of inadequacy that we're not as financially savvy as the people around us.

Mastering your financial confidence marks a profound shift. You're withdrawing from old patterns of behaviour, you're overcoming those inner villains who have been keeping you stuck, you're calling yourself out, you're slowing down to notice how you think, feel and behave with money, and you're following through on promises you make to yourself. You're committing to setting financial boundaries around your behaviour so that you can look after future you, making life easier for yourself when everything else is crumbling, and giving yourself the power to seize opportunities that come to you.

You're entering your Good With Money era

Entering your Good With Money era is like getting a system upgrade. You're you, but better. Safer. More secure. More trusting. You've got more self-belief, more discipline, a greater sense of purpose and a bigger, bolder vision of what's available to you. And that's going to grow over time too, as you commit more and more to your new financial identity.

I want you to take some time here to get creative with the you that's entering their Good With Money era, with the you that's opening doors for future you, with the you that's setting yourself up, and turning your back on behaviours that were making you feel like crap.

It's all about becoming the main character of your finances—that's what happens when you become Good With Money, and as your new financial reality unfolds, your character can evolve even further.

Creating a new money mantra

To mark your entrance to your Good With Money era and to reflect all the work you've done, you can now assign yourself a new money mantra. Unlike the belief rewriting you've done and the shifts to your attitudes and perspectives on money that are underway as part of your system upgrade, your money mantra is a single statement that you can carry with you, in your head or physically on paper (ideally, both!) and recall easily when you're faced with financial challenges.

The aim of your money mantra is to keep your Good With Money attitude top of mind, and unlock the cascade of tools you now have available to help you make better money decisions and engage in the behaviours that leave you feeling more financially confident.

Your money mantra will be unique to you, and will relate to the parts of this book that have connected with you the most, so give yourself some time to come up with something that feels right. The most powerful mantras are ones that speak to the various aspects of your relationship with money, including:

- your financial beliefs
- your worthiness and sense of self
- the way you feel about yourself
- your newly expanded financial window.

Ideas and thought-starters for your money mantra

- I deserve to have money on my side.
- I am enough as I am and I am worthy of holding money for my own choices.
- Money is fun and easy and helps me be my authentic self.
- I call the shots on my money.
- Holding money makes me feel empowered, safe and confident.
- I trust myself with money.

Redefining what money is for

One of the greatest shifts you'll go through when becoming Good With Money is redefining what money is actually for. We've talked a lot about money being a resource that you can deploy in your life in any way you want to, but when you've been financially stuck for a long time, it can be difficult to really understand and embrace that, especially once you break out of those sabotaging habit cycles and find yourself thinking, 'Okay, I've stopped overspending, but what now?'

There's an emerging pocket of research at the intersection of Positive Psychology and financial planning. In a 2015 *Journal of Financial Planning* article, financial planning expert Sarah Asebedo and psychologist Martin Seay explored what financial advice could look like if it shifted from a needs-based approach (that looks to optimise financial outcomes purely in the numerical sense) to involve more of a focus on flourishing and adding value to an individual's life. Flourishing is one of the central components of Positive Psychology, the branch of psychology founded by Martin Seligman we learned about on page 154. It aims to foster joy and wellbeing in order to improve people's lives, rather than just repair them back to baseline.

According to Positive Psychology, there are five key tenets of happiness and wellbeing. These five elements form the PERMA model.

PERMA stands for:

» positive emotions
» engagement
» relationships
» meaning
» achievement.

When we apply the PERMA model to our ongoing approach to financial health, we can redefine the role of money in our lives and explore new ways to use it as a resource to foster happiness in multiple areas of life. The PERMA model pushes us outside of our conditioned beliefs around what makes us happy. This is particularly valuable given everything we explored in Part 1 of this book. With opportunities to consume our way to happiness everywhere we look, a more rounded approach to joy is needed now more than ever.

One of the greatest challenges I believe we face on our money journeys is establishing what does and doesn't make us happy. We have been so conditioned to find happiness in 'stuff' that it's easy to get confused by what we're trying to achieve. On face value, we can justify just about any purchase as using money to make us happy. 'These clothes make me happy,' 'That holiday makes me happy,' 'Eating and drinking out makes me happy.'

And while that might be true to some degree, the PERMA model forces us to look at happiness and wellbeing outside of the consumption-fuelled happiness silo we've come to know.

Let's explore each of the components of PERMA to broaden our view of what makes us happy and explore ways that money can be used to uphold that.

Positive emotions

Positive emotion is the type of happiness we're most familiar with. It's also the one we most often abuse. If I were to make one change to the positive emotions category (not that I'm suggesting that the inventor of Positive Psychology needs or wants my two cents on this!) when applying it to finances in particular, I'd make it *lasting* positive emotion. Or *enduring*.

Or anything that really serves to call out our habitual reliance on instant gratification. There are true positive emotions, and then there are the fleeting positive emotions that come from the surge of dopamine we get when we're spending money. They are not the same. Using money to obtain lasting positive emotions really comes down to that values-based spending we explored in Part 4.

Engagement

Engagement refers to hobbies or activities that we immerse ourselves in and get joy from. This might be gardening, painting, cooking, running, reading, playing a musical instrument, roller skating . . . whatever floats your personal boat.

Relationships

Positive relationships and connection to others are widely known to be important for fostering wellbeing. In a financial sense, money here would be spent on gifting things to people you love or holidaying or dining out with friends, or even investing in building new relationships by getting out and meeting new people.

Meaning

Meaning comes from contributing to a community or being part of something bigger, perhaps volunteering or offering support to someone who needs it. It essentially gives us purpose and a reason for being. It can come from spending time with family, building a meaningful career, or even something like joining a community organisation. Having money means having choices—having financial stability can allow us to make choices that align with having purpose or meaning, like working fewer hours, or choosing a career that's more meaningful than lucrative.

Achievement

Achievement refers to the pursuit of success, mastery or accomplishment. Humans actually have a predisposition for growth and self-actualisation, and so it makes sense that working towards something that improves who we are or develops the self in some way helps us to achieve that central goal of wellbeing. Allowing ourselves to see money as a tool for self-actualisation, perhaps through learning a skill, retraining in a new discipline or traveling the world solo, can build a strong emotional connection between us and our financial behaviour.

It's important to note here that things can straddle multiple elements of the PERMA model. For example, dining out may be in positive emotions and relationships if it's done with others and contributes to the building of meaningful connections.

> **TASK: Audit and aspire**
>
> Using the PERMA model, try what I call an audit and aspire reflection. This is an audit of your life and exploration of your future aspirations. It can be helpful in assessing where your money is allocated now (or where it's perhaps lacking application) and how you could aspire to use it in the future.
>
> Here's an example audit of current behaviour and potential behaviour to aspire to.

	AUDIT: how you use your money now	**ASPIRE: how you could aspire to use money in the future**
Positive emotions	Morning coffee, clothing, cocktails, skincare, accessories	Buy less clothing but higher quality, keep your morning coffee, get a regular facial, have a stylist
Engagement	Occasional reading	Regularly reading fiction books (two per month), taking daily walks in nature, visiting the beach, sewing
Relationships	Dining/drinking out	Monthly date night or group dinner, regular weekend breaks to reconnect, special dinner out with family each week, hiring a cleaner to free up family time on weekends, gifting or giving time/support to those who matter to you
Meaning	None	Volunteering with local animal shelter, donating to causes that matter to you and doing pro-bono work
Achievement	Ad hoc gym visits, reading self-development books	Running a marathon, writing a book, learning new cooking skills, improving strength and health with Pilates, continuing to read personal development books, taking a course, learning a language

The PERMA model is just one way of adopting a more holistic, zoomed-out view of how your money can enrich your life.

We often get stuck in the viewpoint of just focusing on the things we can consume, and leaving out all the other possibilities that money could allow us to explore. This type of audit and aspire work can also help us see where redeploying some of the money we spend on the easiest to access positive emotions category could open up opportunities in other areas.

Ongoing work on your money beliefs and financial comfort zone

There's a big part of getting Good With Money that's about healing the past, undoing patterns of behaviour and rebuilding your money mindset from the ground up. The exploratory work we've done together will go a long way in helping you understand your patterns of behaviour and how to achieve better outcomes by intercepting these cycles.

Improving our mindsets around money is an ongoing process, and we're stretching our financial comfort zone as we go. Our beliefs, behaviours and experiences are a three-legged stool—when one changes, the other two change too.

» As we work on changing our beliefs, our behaviours and experiences change in alignment with that.

» As we work on changing our behaviours, our beliefs and experiences change in alignment with that.

» As we change our financial experiences (e.g. our financial outcomes), our beliefs and behaviours change in alignment with that.

Over time, these gradual shifts from small actions can help you develop a more positive relationship with money and a more positive financial experience. As you do so, your financial comfort zone can slowly stretch as you become more familiar with things like healthy spending behaviours, holding money in savings and making financial decisions that are in your best interest.

That's not to say we won't ever run into bumps in the road. As our financial outlooks improve, we can run into beliefs that may have previously been dormant, or old beliefs can be reactivated by new experiences that might be similar to negative experiences we've had in the past.

Before I got Good With Money, I was a hot money mess. I never saw a future where I'd be able to have savings or cover unexpected expenses or feel in control of my finances in any way.

The work I did to change that—to get myself out of debt, to build up savings and to relearn how to spend money in a healthy way—was momentous. I changed my beliefs, my behaviour and my experiences and outcomes gradually, through small, consistent actions, and it felt great.

The problem was, I had adjusted my money mindset and stretched my financial comfort zone to get me there—but no further. One of the most unexpected parts of my financial journey was having to re-look at my beliefs after I had unlocked a new level of financial confidence, in order to unlock the next one. For me, that was moving beyond paying off debt and having a small amount of savings. To get to the point where I had more savings and could start thinking about taking control of my finances on a bigger scale, I had to undergo another system upgrade. My dreams of having some savings and being out of debt had been realised, but I had no further dreams.

Outside of your beliefs and your comfort zone, you're also going to run into change and adversity in life, and money will almost always be directly or indirectly related to those experiences. Redundancy, injury or illness, failures, relationship breakdowns, divorce, grief—all of these things can impact the way we feel about money. Some of us encounter more of these challenges than others, and what comes our way is almost impossible to predict. But I have to prepare you for the fact that new 'money stuff' can come up in life even after you've gotten Good With Money.

We need to be prepared to undergo another mini system upgrade every time our financial or life circumstances change, in order to keep stretching that financial comfort zone and reprogramming the way we think, feel and behave to align to that new reality.

Life changes that can impact your money mindset are:

» getting a higher salary
» coming into money (e.g. through a bonus, inheritance or other windfall)
» taking a career change or break that impacts your earnings
» starting a business
» a change in the way you earn money (e.g. if you go from a base pay rate to a commission or bonus structure)
» a change in your expenses
» a change in your role in life, e.g. becoming a parent
» starting or ending a relationship
» buying a home
» investing in the stock market
» becoming ill or experiencing an injury
» being made redundant
» bereavement or loss.

Really, anything that either has the potential to change your financial position, for better or worse, or that causes your brain to recall a previous financial flashpoint.

When I left my job in 2021 to become self-employed full time, the impact on my money mindset was profound. It took me a long time to realise it, but I'd only upgraded my system within the confines of employment. Within the security of a regular income, within the predictability of having a traditional job that paid a wage and, interestingly, within the boundaries of the relatively crap salaries that came with the industry I was working in.

I hadn't realised it, but I'd been existing in a comfort zone that was created by the fact it was fairly unlikely I'd ever earn a high salary. You might experience this if you work in an industry that keeps your pay grades fairly static—you might simply have never entertained the idea that you could be one of those people who earned great money or who could experience financial success.

Becoming self-employed, however, presented a series of challenges that threatened my financial mindset.

» Income wasn't ever guaranteed, and the uncertainty of that hit a nerve with the instability I'd experienced back when I was a hot money mess. The inconsistency made me feel like I'd backslid and undone all my hard work.

» While income wasn't guaranteed, there was also no ceiling. People around me were talking about earning much bigger numbers, sharing experiences of how quickly things could change (in a good way and a bad way), and my proximity to higher incomes felt closer than ever.

» It also meant that to get that big money, I had to trust myself. I had to be confident, I had to ask for what I wanted, I had to believe I was worth more money, and I had to slap that price on my work. Having always felt fairly confident in my ability to do my day job, the lack of confidence I experienced in business was a real slap in the face to my financial mindset.

The experience of self-employment really activated my old beliefs, uncovered new ones, and challenged some of the positive changes I'd made when I was just wanting to get out of debt and have some savings. Essentially, I had to adjust to a new identity, look out for how that adjustment was affecting my financial beliefs and behaviour, and learn to experience money in a new way. To be honest, some of that is still a work in progress as I write!

None of this is say you have to start the whole Good With Money process again—don't panic! But part of being Good With Money is adjusting and upgrading your money mindset as you move through life. It might be that a new belief comes up, or that you need to accommodate new expenses, or an old behaviour resurfaces that you want to work on reprogramming. You can revisit any of the techniques in this book whenever you need to tighten up your habits, beliefs or behaviours. The money mindfulness techniques below will also become an important part of managing your money mindset.

Money won't be linear

Our growth won't be linear in a mathematical sense (unless we get really, *really* lucky), and definitely not in a mindset sense. We won't always have more money coming in than we did last year. We won't always have more in savings than we did last month. We

> have to get comfortable with the ups and downs of life and how they impact our finances, and be okay with being further behind than where we were, either by chance, if bad luck has come our way, or by choice, if we've made the decision to start a business or change careers or become a parent.

Money mindfulness

Now that you're Good With Money (wink), you already have an awareness of how your thoughts, feelings and beliefs can impact your behaviour and your financial experience. This awareness alone will help you if you run into roadblocks as your financial situation changes.

Having somewhere to use that awareness is where real change can happen. Mindfulness techniques for your money can be helpful in addressing any shifts or challenges facing your mindset around money, particularly when encountering any of the life changes we talked about earlier. Going into a change to your financial situation, no matter how good or bad, with an awareness that you may hit up against some toxic money beliefs is a great first step. You'll be well positioned to explore any feelings that present themselves.

Money belief log
When you're experiencing a financial or life change or your 'money stuff' seems to be a little bit off, carrying out a money belief log can be really helpful in making sense of your thoughts and feelings.

Keeping track of the thoughts you have about money and the context in which they're occuring can help you uncover what's getting in your way. You can then counter that with a more positive or neutral thought to help you move forward.

You might want to use a note-taking app on your phone to jot down thoughts and feelings that come up about money in real time, and revisit them after a week or month to see what patterns are presenting.

Financial journalling

Journalling has been proven to help you make sense of messy thoughts or feelings by helping you access your subconscious mind and bring things into your consciousness by setting them out on a page in front of you. You can journal about all kinds of things, but carving out time to journal specifically on financial matters can be really beneficial when it comes to ensuring toxic financial beliefs don't resurface or evolve.

> **TASK**
>
> ## Making sense of your money beliefs
>
> Here are some journal prompts to get you thinking, some to help you navigate adversity, and some to help you think bigger.
>
> *Overcoming adversities*
> - What's stopping you from achieving your full financial potential right now?
> - If your financial problem were a person and you were going to scream at them, what would you say?

- If your money were a person, what would you want to say to them right now?
- If someone were to come and help you with money right now, what would that look like and why?
- If you could wake up tomorrow and have this problem solved, what would your life look like and how would you know the problem was sorted?

Dreaming big, setting goals, making money feel good
- If you were given $1,000 on the condition that you had to use it to enrich your life in some way, what would you spend it on and how would you make a compelling case for its use?
- What do you love about money?
- What choices do you dream of having in the future?
- Describe what your ideal day looks like.
- Write out five reasons why you're worthy and deserving of financial confidence.
- Write a letter to yourself a year from now.
- Write a letter to yourself from one year ago.
- How can you use money to deeply care for yourself in your life?
- What does money make possible for you?
- What's something you've achieved with money that you're really proud of? Describe it and own that success.
- Imagine yourself as someone you love (a friend or family member) and write them a letter telling them how proud you are of everything they've achieved.

Building financial resilience

Being Good With Money is about more than having 'good days'. We don't want to only feel good about money when everything's smooth sailing. We want to build a robust mindset that can stand the test of life getting in the way.

Money is one of life's great stressors. Even if you're Good With Money, you're not immune to financial stress. In fact, even if you're incredibly wealthy, you're not immune to financial stress either! Financial stress and anxiety will scale with you if you don't develop a level of resilience.

There is a growing body of research around the importance of resilience and how we can develop as resilient individuals, and much of this thinking can be applied to our finances as well.

When it comes to money, we require two types of resilience: mental or emotional resilience, and financial resilience. The two can work together to help us weather difficult financial impacts.

Mental resilience

When we encounter unexpected financial impacts, we feel threatened. And as we know, our brain's immediate response is to try to keep us safe by creating meaning around those threats. The problem here is that often this meaning is misplaced. In attempting to make sense of financial adversity, we can spiral into catastrophic thinking, enact crisis plans or even sabotage our finances altogether.

As an example, imagine you're making progress with your money ecosystem, you're starting to build up savings and seeing changes as a result of your efforts. Then, you find yourself faced with an unexpected expense, like a bill for car repairs that requires you to use your savings. Your default response here might be to feel angry and spiral into patterns of thinking like 'What's the point in even trying?' or back to beliefs like 'No matter what I do, money will always be stressful.'

Referring back once more to the field of Positive Psychology, learned optimism has been suggested as a mechanism for improving our response to less-than-ideal outcomes. There are three cognitive distortions that affect the way we view and respond to adversity. These are known as the three Ps: permanence, pervasiveness and personalisation.

- **Permanence** refers to the duration we associate with an incident of adversity.

- **Pervasiveness** refers to the way we ascribe either specific or universal effects and meanings to such an incident.

» **Personalisation** refers to our attribution of cause or blame for the incident, either to internal or external factors.

When we're experiencing financial stress, these cognitive distortions affect the way we make sense of what's happened. Let's take an example of getting served the bad luck of $3,000 in car repairs out of the blue.

Permanence

We either see the car bill bad luck as an isolated incident, or we see it as a piece of a bigger picture about our financial outlook. Our narratives here might be things like:

'This is unfortunate, we need to find that $3,000 by [insert viable solutions here]'—an isolated, temporary incident.

'Ughhh, of course this happens now, I knew this would happen, this means we won't be able to go on holiday or do this or do that'—a broader, permanent problem.

Pervasiveness

'We'll be dipping into the emergency fund this month, but we'll get it back to where it needs to be'—a specific incident concerning one thing.

'Everything's ruined, money is so bloody hard, I don't know why I bother trying'—a universal problem.

Personalisation

'I did what I could to be prepared for those repairs but who could've known they'd be that much?'—external attribution.

'I should have been more prepared, I wish I hadn't spent money on that last week or been on that nice holiday, I should've prevented this'—self-blame.

Mental resilience when it comes to our finances is all down to the meaning we attribute to our experiences. Being able to intercept thought spirals and see where we're extrapolating something to fit what our brains want to believe is an incredibly powerful skill, and over time as our relationships with money improve and our toxic beliefs are replaced with more positive ones, the way we experience money feels more in our control.

You can work on your mental resilience by keeping track of the way you make sense of micro moments on your financial journey, and noticing how the three Ps present themselves in the stories your brain makes up.

» Are you stretching what's happened to make it mean something about you or your potential?

» Are you blaming yourself for something that was out of your control?

» Are you writing off longer-term goals or plans because of something that's only temporary?

To be clear: mental resilience isn't about toxic positivity. It's not about telling yourself things are great when they're not. Financial difficulty can't be fixed by thinking positively, and those who suggest it can are spruiking a dangerous narrative. Mental resilience is about neutralising and isolating an experience so you can see it for what it is and what it is only, rather than creating a new story to uphold beliefs that keep you stuck.

Financial resilience

Financial resilience comes from setting up our finances to mitigate risk and bolster impact. Things like emergency savings and access to resources and support when we need it. Some of us have more baked-in financial resilience than others, and privilege plays an important role here.

Fostering financial resilience can directly feed into your mental resilience around your finances. If you know the building blocks of support are there for you, you're able to reason when your threat-responsive brain starts doing mental gymnastics.

Let's explore some of the key components of financial resilience and how you can work on dialling up your access to each.

Components of financial resilience
- positive habits
- awareness and engagement (e.g. what your base costs are)
- contingency plans (e.g. savings, social capital)
- experience in handling financial adversity.

Positive habits, awareness and engagement

The habits we've explored in this book, from reclaiming your financial decisions to creating your financial ecosystem, to the awareness of where your temptations come from, will help with your financial resilience.

Part of financial resilience is knowing how to act in a crisis and being somewhat prepared for it. If financial stress is going to strike, would you prefer it to happen when your finances are chaotic and messy and you're constantly trying to start over and take control, or when you've got your ducks in a row, your habits in check and your ecosystem set up? I know which I'd prefer.

If you're in control of your money and you have a system for it, working out where to go next when adversity strikes is substantially easier. Plus, you know you've done what you can to put yourself in a position to handle the challenge effectively.

Contingency plans (access to support and resources)

Our contingency plans really come from what we'll do if we can't fix the problem by adjusting our budgets. We can never know what exactly is going to happen, but while some financial impacts can be weathered by shifting where our money goes for a period of time or cutting back on a certain category, larger impacts require us to access money from elsewhere.

This is going to be things like our emergency fund. The bigger our emergency fund, the stronger our financial resilience.

The next step after our emergency funds is going to be any other savings. Yes, if we've set aside money for travel or big dreams or a car, in an ideal world we don't touch it, but if it can mean the difference between getting through a financial stressor or not, sometimes we have to readjust our priorities.

Your own level of social capital also plays into your contingency plan. Do you have family you can borrow money from? If you need somewhere to stay, can you move back home, or do you have siblings you can live with? How about your friends? Do they have enough space (physical and mental) for you to stay with them? This is where privilege really plays a part in your financial resilience.

Everyone's situation is different. And while you can't plan for every scenario, giving some thought to your options if you do experience financial difficulty can help you withstand unexpected challenges, and dial up your commitment to your financial future in the process.

Experience in handling financial adversity
The last component of your financial resilience is experience in navigating negative impacts. Every time you deal with a financial curveball and get through the other side, your resilience increases. It's the same in life. The more you've experienced, the more resilient you are. Knowing that you can get through a tough time and rebuild on the other side is incredibly powerful.

Cultivating a positive relationship with money

To have a positive relationship with money, we need to treat it right. We need to look after it when it comes to us. We need to do what we say we're going to do. We need to think about where it'll flourish, and where it can do its best work.

Money is a resource that helps us manage our worlds and flourish in our lives. Money is an employee of our business of life and it's our job to maximise its value like a true leader.

Think about a boss you've not liked. What were their qualities? Maybe they micro-managed you. Maybe they talked badly about you or they were never there when you needed them. Maybe you'd show up and give it your all, only to be ignored or dismissed.

Without realising it, we can slip into the role of a toxic boss when it comes to our money. We micro-manage it, ignore it, demand too much of it, we don't allow it to grow and evolve with our business of life or we overwork it and cause it to burn out.

How to not be a toxic boss to your money

Treating your money with respect

We all want to be respected by our managers, and money is no different. When we respect money, we don't project our own emotions onto it. We don't expect too much of it. We don't ignore it or belittle it. We understand it's there to do a job, one that it's great at by the way, and we set up the systems to let it do its thing. When we respect our money, we respect ourselves.

Respecting your money can look like:

» following through on plans to save it
» spending it on things you value
» prioritising it in line with what matters most
» meeting your needs first, and adding your wants later
» paying yourself first (see page 225).

Open and honest communication

We want our relationship with money to feel like a mutual exchange, like we're doing what we can to support money and money is doing its best to support us. Sometimes there will be issues that need to be worked through, but when we can sit down and tackle those challenges, set a plan, make compromises if necessary and forge a path forward through adversity, we can expect far better outcomes than if we were to shut down and avoid the problem.

Opportunities for growth

Lots of us want to grow in our jobs, and so does money! Yep, money is an ambitious little beast. It wants to upskill, it wants to grow with our business of life, it wants to play to its strengths and be able to serve us better. When we honour these wants, we allow money to evolve in new ways as we grow. We allow it to serve new needs within our business of life, and we realise its value in new and different applications.

Early in our partnership, money might be at the entry-level stage of chipping away at a savings goal. Later in life, it might start working on wealth-creation behaviours. Then maybe it might support us to realise a dream. If we let money grow and evolve with us and our business of life, we can enjoy the outcomes of our joint input.

Letting money do its thing

Nobody likes a micro-manager, so don't be one to your money. Money needs a degree of autonomy just like you do. Setting up your financial ecosystem (and tweaking it where necessary) gives money the chance to do its thing FOR YOU. You don't need to watch over every single cent in order to be steering the ship.

Other important factors that go into cultivating a positive relationship with money

Enjoying money

Yes, when you're Good With Money, you get to *enjoy* your money! Making sure you're doing exactly that is critical to feeling good about money long term. But allowing yourself to use money to enrich your life is actually harder than it sounds.

Often you think you're doing this when you're living on autopilot and passively spending your money on things you think make you happy. But enjoying your money when you're Good With Money is about intentionality. Make sure your financial ecosystem (see page 218) is set up to accommodate some enjoyment, and revisit the joy-ranking exercise (see page 134) to keep an eye on how much pleasure you're getting from your money.

Allowing yourself to spend money on the things you know enrich your life is a learning curve, but you've done some great foundational work already. Continuing to unpack your financial values, recalibrating what you actually want (not what you've been conditioned to want) and paying close attention to where money can be best deployed in your life is critical to building on that positive relationship with money.

The bottom line: you CAN spend money! In fact, that's the point!

Knowing where your money is going

Remember when we looked at the difference between active and passive money management back on page 213? That active component of knowing where your money is going is really important when building a positive relationship with it. When you know where your money goes, you're automatically more in control.

You don't need to be perfect to have a positive relationship with money. You just need to maintain a level of control and confidence that means you're able to course-correct if things do slip.

Thinking about money more positively

Ah, those pesky thoughts again. Why is it always my bloody thoughts? The way you think about money *is* really important, though, sorry to say it. Maintaining a healthy (not toxically positive, but *healthy*) money mindset will help your relationship with money grow. Imagine again that money is a person you're in a relationship with. A constant fear of the relationship breaking down, or constant worrying about the future of the relationship, is going to put a strain on it. The same goes with your relationship with money.

Those beliefs we've talked about are the biggest ongoing component of being Good With Money. Noticing when toxic thoughts are creeping in and being ready for some wacky thoughts and feelings to come up when your life situation changes.

This can be as simple as taking a moment to recognise how you've been feeling about money at the end of each day or week, and practising reframing some of your money thoughts and beliefs in the same way you did on pages 140–156. You might already be familiar with gratitude practices—for example, writing down three things you're grateful for at the end of each day. Recognising and reframing your money thoughts can work in a similar way, by leveraging the benefits of neuroplasticity to gradually shift your perspective over time.

Earning more, building wealth and creating a life of freedom

In Part 1, we talked about how women have continually been not only left out of financial conversations, but directly distracted from achieving financial success. Instead of being taught about markets, stocks and wealth creation like our male counterparts, we were sold cellulite creams and warned about the impacts of ageing. All of that conveniently routed any money we did have right back into the hands of corporations.

I addressed at the beginning of this book that being Good With Money doesn't solve for the myriad financial inequities we experience in the world. What it does do is form a foundational level of financial participation, confidence and understanding, off of which we can launch to achieve more than we might have been able to otherwise.

What the world needs is more money in the hands of women—and being Good With Money puts you in a great position to get it. I want you to take your newfound financial confidence and use it to go and earn more money, keep more money and make that money work harder for you.

If you're not Good With Money, earning more of it won't change all that much. It's why we hear that the majority of lottery winners end up back where they started, or of professional sportspeople earning millions of dollars during their career and still having to work after retirement. Building good habits, understanding the stories your brain makes up about money and confronting those toxic beliefs that get in the way are crucial steps to take before you earn more money. But once you are Good With Money, the next level is to get more of it—and manage the crap out of that too!

Earning more money

Put simply, more money gives you more choices. More options. More opportunities. Something people commonly say about money is, 'Oh, I just want to have enough.' Humble, right? The problem with 'enough' is that it's unquantifiable. Enough . . . for what? Enough to one person isn't enough to another, because one person's definition of a simple life isn't another's.

So regardless of whether you want a big, sparkly, shiny life of city living, global travel, champagne and spare bedrooms or a quiet, rural life on the land, growing your own veggies and joining the PTA (neither is superior to the other, by the way), you still need to quantify what it is you're after, and put the wheels in motion to get you there.

Having choices is one of the most valuable things to any human being in this world. The problem is, not all money creates the type of choices we want. If we strive only for money, we might earn it in a way that doesn't give us the choices we want. Likewise, some choices require more money than others, and we don't want to get caught up in grasping for more and more and more when actually we could have had the choices we wanted two mores ago, but missed them because we were so focused on amassing as much wealth as possible.

You can't grow wealth without one thing: investing

Unfortunately, earning more money simply isn't enough when it comes to building wealth over the long term. When you earn money and split it between spending and keeping, the portion that you keep can only grow so far. When your money is in a savings account it earns interest, which means the financial institution pays you a percentage of your balance every year to keep your money there. Sounds great, right? Except it doesn't account for inflation.

Inflation is the rising cost of goods and services (which you are probably very familiar with given our recent economic turbulence!). Governments generally want inflation to rise steadily, as it's the sign of a growing economy. The problem for your savings account comes when inflation is higher than the interest rate you're being paid. Say the financial institution has paid you three per cent on your $10,000 savings, but inflation has pushed the price of goods and services up by four per cent; your money is worth less than it was before, even with extra money earned via that three per cent interest.

So if all you do is save your money, it can't grow at the pace you need it to in order to outpace your costs of living and allow you the choices you want in life. But what you can do is invest some of your savings into assets that grow in value at a faster rate.

> When you invest in an asset, it can help you grow your money in two ways. Firstly, it can grow in value, so you can buy it at one price and sell it at a higher price. The second way is through the asset earning you income while you own it. For example, owning a property and charging rent for people to live in it, or earning a dividend (which is a share of company profits) when you own a share in a business.
>
> Now, that's not to say you shouldn't be saving. The fact that your savings can lose a little value along the way is irrelevant. You can't be growing all your money all the time. But after gaining a certain level of financial security through saving (which comes from being Good With Money), you unlock an opportunity to grow any further surplus of money.
>
> Now, investing might sound like a no-brainer, but it comes with risk. When invested, your money can grow, but it's not guaranteed to grow. In fact, it can lose value. Where your money in a savings account is protected and can't drop in value, investments can (and will) fluctuate during the time that you own them, and they need to be approached with caution.

Get acquainted with wealth

The word 'wealth' itself carries some pretty icky connotations, thanks to money-hoarding billionaires who insist on exploiting people for the simple reason of amassing more and more money.

But there is wealth that isn't corruption. There is wealth that isn't sickening greed. So what I want you to do here is to let go of what you think about wealth, what you know about wealth and what you feel about wealth. You have to let go of that as the sole idea of wealth if you want to be able to achieve any semblance of it for yourself.

I want you to start thinking of wealth as a choice. Right from being able to choose to buy the expensive mayonnaise in the store, up to being able to choose to take six months off work, to being able to work a lower-paying job because you enjoy it more, to being able to see someone in need and help them, to being able to give time and money to causes you care about.

> **TASK**
>
> ## What does wealth mean to you?
>
> Let's get more personal. I want you to start defining what wealth can mean for you, at all different levels. Start with the choices you'd like to have in your life. What do you really want? What options would you love to have? What freedom would you love to have? What would you do if money were no issue?
>
> Refer back to your financial values from pages 191–203.
>
> Refer back to your PERMA model from pages 272–277.
>
> Pull them together to capture an idea of what wealth can mean for you. Take this as permission to dream big here—but keep it grounded in your values and your responses to the PERMA model. It's easy to just shove in everything we've been conditioned to want, flash holidays and beachfront houses and designer bags and business-class flights and luxury sofas and those signature outward displays of wealth. If those things feel right to you, that's absolutely fine, but try to deeply explore wealth not just through what you want to buy, but through the lenses of choice, freedom and opportunity.

- What options do you want to have in life?
- What does wealth mean for you outside of 'stuff'?
- How do you want to spend your time?
- Who do you want to spend your time with?
- Why do you want these things?
- How do you want to experience life?

Sometimes it's tempting to go wild here, but what actually happens when we paint a picture of wealth that isn't true to us is that we create more psychological distance between us and that wealth, because it doesn't ultimately mean anything to us. We're not going to make sacrifices or take risks to work towards something we don't truly want. We need to have a view of wealth and potential grounded in what matters to us in order for it to stick.

The relationship between money and time

We've all heard that old saying 'Time is money, my friend,' usually barked by a boss to an employee, or smugly and sneeringly said by a stockbroker on a Wall Street trading floor. Slimy dudes aside, time and money are inextricably linked, particularly when we're talking about your future growth.

In a capitalist society, we have to spend a large portion of our time earning money to pay our basic needs. We're also entirely responsible for bearing the costs of unpredictable life events like health incidents, the repair of resources (e.g. homes or cars), etc. Generally these things take precedence over the 'add-ons' that bring us joy. In fact, I believe part of the reason we often over-index the positive emotions experienced through discretionary spending or material things is due to the lack of time we have to dedicate to experiencing joy or fulfilment in other categories.

When we're time-poor, it's more viable for us to find joy in placing an online order than it is to find joy from spending four hours gardening. When we leave for work in the dark and return eight to ten hours later also in the dark, it's no wonder we struggle to engage with other paths to joy.

But money can buy us time and reduce our reliance on the proportion of our time that gets spent on covering our basic needs, opening up opportunities for joy simply through freeing up time. For example, you might have always wanted to volunteer but wondered how it's possible when you work full-time hours with unpaid overtime and can't even deal with your own responsibilities, let alone someone else's.

When we have access to more money, we can buy the time we need to deploy into things that bring us joy. While this might be out of reach in the present, the idea of money signifiying time can help us form goals and visions of the ideal life we'd like to lead, where perhaps we work part time or take a less demanding job so we can have more energy and free time on the weekends to do those things that would bring us joy.

What I'm saying is you might not need money to do the thing, but you might need money to buy you the time to do the thing.

That's where wealth creation really comes into it. I've said it before—being Good With Money isn't the end of the journey; it's the beginning. It will give you freedom from the stress and stuckness that comes with never making any meaningful financial progress. The next step after that is the freedom that allows you to outsmart the systems keeping you stuck, and reclaim your life through financial growth and independence.

> ### Don't forget your financial window
>
> While thinking too big is a risk here, thinking too small or in terms that are too limited can also be a risk. Don't forget your financial window: if you don't know what's possible, it's harder to see it as accessible to you. You might need to spend some time thinking deeply about the choices you've never let yourself dream could be possible, or even come up with things that you've never known anyone else to do.
>
> You might be the first person in your family to engage in wealth-creation behaviours and that can be confronting, for you and for your relatives. Your old financial comfort zone can be partly upheld by generational patterns and limitations in economic mobility, and breaking out of these cycles can be emotional. Working on seeking out evidence to positively support your decision to pursue wealth can be helpful in moving through these feelings.

How to go from getting Good With Money to building wealth

I've said it before: reclaiming your spending decisions, building your financial ecosystem and getting in control of your money won't make you wealthy. But they are the first steps. You can't go off investing money and trying to grow wealth if your finances are still all over the place. (Well, you can, you can do whatever you like, but it's rarely recommended!)

I'm going to take you through the stages of wealth-building and where we go from here.

Step 1: unpack your beliefs and behaviours (which you've ticked off by reading this book, yay!)

Understanding your past, identifying your inner villains, opening your financial window, getting in control of your money, learning how to save, relearning how to spend, cutting out spending on things that don't matter to you and getting intentional with the way you consume—that's getting Good With Money.

Step 2: squash consumer debt

If you have any consumer debt, credit cards, personal loans, car loans (really anything that isn't a mortgage or a student loan), prioritise paying these off before moving forward with building wealth. The simple reason is that consumer debt carries interest rates that can reach upward of twenty per cent. Investing to grow your wealth generally won't earn you more than the twenty per cent you're paying on that debt, so clearing it first will give you the best bang for your buck.

Step 3: build up emergency savings and financial resilience

You don't want to be investing in anything with any level of risk (which is all investments) until you have your financial resilience nailed down. You need to have ready access to money before you can start taking any risks, so make sure you've got healthy emergency savings set aside first.

Step 4: grow your money

Once those three things are ticked off, you can confidently start engaging in wealth-creation behaviours. That's going to involve investing in things that grow your money faster than you can yourself. You can invest in the stock market, in property, in your retirement fund (which you likely already have in the form of your superannuation), or in other assets that have the potential to grow in value or earn you money.

Your wealth-creation journey may also involve boosting the money you earn, either by increasing your salary, or by bringing in money on the side. If you're self-employed, it'll involve growing your profit. The more money you earn, the more you can put towards growing your wealth.

One thing I want you to remember, though, is that it's not so significant how much you earn, but how much you keep. Remember how my unhelpful belief that I could always earn more money actually drove me to spend more? It's important that extra money earned is used in the right way. You want to be increasing the gap between your income and your expenses—that's where the power is. You can earn $300,000 a year, but if you're spending $280,000 of it you're no better off than someone earning $40,000 and only spending $20,000.

You can either increase this gap by earning more money (yeehaw) and sending that extra surplus towards your future, or by reducing your expenses. Earning money is generally seen to be easier, but it really does depend on your situation. Instead of focusing solely on increasing income, focus on that gap, because it can open up your creativity when it comes to wealth creation.

Some specific ways to increase the gap between your income and expenses, from simple, obvious options to more creative strategies, include:

- increasing your salary at your full-time job and directing the surplus all or partly towards wealth creation
- starting a profitable business on the side or taking on side jobs and investing all the money you make as it comes in
- moving back in with your family (if this is an option you have) to save most of your income for a short period of time and investing that surplus
- taking a job that drastically reduces your living expenses, for example, remote work with accommodation provided, seasonal roles during ski seasons, or other incentivised relocations
- taking a job that offers you a temporarily inflated income for a short period of time, before returning to your usual job and routine, for example, a teacher taking on relief work for a year along with another side job to maximise income-earning opportunities
- moving to a region, city or country with much lower costs of living and paring back your lifestyle to direct more money into saving and investing.

Resources to help you get started investing to build wealth

I wanted to introduce you to the concept of wealth creation and growing your money further because it's the next step after getting Good With Money and taking control of your finances. But, aside from needing an entire other book to go into detail, it's also not my specialty. There are other incredible women who contribute so much knowledge, insight and perspective to the financial conversation specifically about investing and building wealth, and so it's time now for me to direct you to their work.

The resources listed below are some of my favourite places to learn about growing your money.

Girls That Invest

Led by Simran Kaur and Sonya Gupthan, Girls That Invest has become a destination empowering women to grow their money through investing. Learn from them in their book *Girls That Invest*, listen to the Girls That Invest podcast, or find them on social media @girlsthatinvest.

Natasha Etschmann

Tash has been investing from a young age and teaches others to do the same. Find her on social media @tashinvests, or listen to her podcast, Get Rich Slow Club.

Her First 100K

Founded by Tori Dunlap, Her First 100K is a platform that empowers women to build financial freedom. Read Tori's book *Financial Feminist*, listen to the Financial Feminist podcast, or find her on social media @herfirst100k.

We Should All Be Millionaires

This book by Rachel Rodgers is a woman's guide to earning more, building wealth and gaining economic power. You can also find Rachel on social media @rachelrodgers.

RASK Education

RASK is an educational media platform empowering Australians to build financial freedom. The team offers a range of free and paid courses, and hosts three podcasts: The Australian Finance Podcast, The Australian Business Podcast and The Australian Property Podcast. Find them on social media @raskaustralia.

Go out there and be Good With Money!

You freaking did it! You made it to the end of your Good With Money system upgrade, and you're ready to get out in the world and put all of your learnings into practice. Remember, getting Good With Money isn't something that happens overnight. It's a muscle you'll grow over time as you get more familiar with the perspectives, techniques and shifts we've gone through in this book. If you implement what you've learned during our time together, gradually, you'll start to notice that money feels easier and managing it seems to flow more smoothly. A big part of being Good With Money is striking that balance between being connected enough to money that you care about it, and disconnected enough that you're not watching every single dollar.

It's my hope that this book will have got you thinking differently about your relationship with money, and given you a better understanding of how you can experience money differently. You may find yourself wanting to refer back to parts of the book as you encounter these themes in your real life, and I'd encourage you to do that. Sometimes you can understand something conceptually, but see things differently when you're actually experiencing it.

To give you a quick recap of the key aspects of what it takes to be Good With Money, here are the five most important things to focus on when taking control of your finances:

- **Habits**—creating repetition in your positive behaviour, building a sense of trust that you're making good money decisions, and taking an active role in your finances.
- **Motivation**—connecting to the value money can offer you and retaining that emotional connection to your finances.
- **Identity**—making positive financial behaviour and perspectives part of who you are, and consistently aligning your finances to the things you learn about yourself.
- **Beliefs**—fostering positive, healthy money beliefs that are conducive to positive financial behaviour, and developing a sense of optimism and resilience when it comes to money.
- **Toolkit**—the ecosystem in which your money actually exists, where it goes when it hits your account, and the boundaries and organisational systems you set around your cashola.

Whenever anything doesn't feel quite right in your finances, come back to these five components. Spend some time with each one and see if you can find what's slipping. Being able to respond to cracks that emerge with your money stuff is a powerful skill. Embrace it.

I want you to feel SO FREAKING PROUD of yourself for completing this book. I'm proud of you! Tackling your money stuff isn't easy, but you've made some serious progress over the last 300-odd pages. I cannot wait to hear how you apply the principles from this book to your life and your finances, so shoot me an email or a DM next time you use a framework, confront one of your inner villains, walk away from a sneaky advertising message that almost got you or notice your savings account juicing up as a product of your Good With Money ecosystem.

You deserve to feel like you're getting value from your money. You deserve to trust yourself to earn and manage higher amounts of money. You deserve to decide where your money goes. And you deserve to use money to enjoy your life.

**Let's keep the Good With Money fun going.
You can find me at:**

Instagram: @the.brokegeneration

TikTok: @the.brokegeneration

Email: hello@thebrokegeneration.com

Website: thebrokegeneration.com

Acknowledgements

Wow, where do I even begin. I'm sure I'm not the first person to say this, but not only does it take a village to raise a child, it also takes a village to produce a book!

Firstly, thank you to my husband for being by my side and showing me that unconditional love and support really does exist—even when I'm ugly crying and yelling 'this book is awful!' You've been there for me, not only for the writing of this book, but for the last ten years as I became the person I had to be to write it. There have been many, many, *many* tears during this process, and enough muffled cries of 'I don't think I can do this' to last me a lifetime. But you've always been there to remind me that I can. Turns out you were right. How annoying.

To my publishing team—thank you for taking a chance on me. Tessa, you've been my support for the last eighteen months, calming me during my panicked emails and countless meltdowns, talking to me on Teams for hours until I got the clarity I needed. From the bottom of my heart, thank you for everything. Greer—I've lost count of the times I've started an email with 'sorry I'm such a pain!' Thank you for your work. This book would not exist without you. To the rest of the Allen & Unwin team: Libby,

Emily, Sandra, Allegra and all the other people who touched this book behind the scenes. You're all incredible people.

To my business work wives: Peta, Dani, Annelise, Tash, Victoria—you've listened to my unhinged four-minute voice notes, given me pep talks, dragged me off the edge of despair and reminded me that I'm a bad bitch and I've got this. I am so grateful you are in my life and so thankful for your support.

To my fellow authors Alice, Iolanthe, Ana—your advice got me through the wobbles. And to my friends who have continued to check in on me, let me vent, reminded me I can do this, reminded me to be proud of myself—you've kept me going over the last year and a half.

To Brad and Ted Klontz, my lecturers at Creighton University, and the team at the Financial Psychology Institute—learning from you enriched my perspective on why we do the things we do with money. Thank you for pushing this field forward.

And lastly, thank you all of YOU. Every like, comment, share, read, click, listen and watch has contributed to the existence of this book and the creation of this opportunity for me. I will never not be grateful for all the people I've never met who take the time to read my work and let me know when they've enjoyed it. You know who you are.

One very final acknowledgement, though this may seem strange, goes to some of my favourite fiction authors: Shari Low, Ross King, Patricia Wolf, Yomi Adegoki and Nicola Moriarty. Devouring their novels truly got me through some of my toughest days during this process. Now more than ever, I am endlessly grateful for their work.